A DREAM WITH A DEADLINE

A DREAM WITH A DEADLINE

TURNING STRATEGY INTO ACTION

Jacques Horovitz with Anne-Valérie Ohlsson-Corboz

Prentice Hall
FINANCIAL TIMES

An imprint of **Pearson Education**

Harlow, England • London • New York • Boston • San Francisco • Toronto
Sydney • Tokyo • Singapore • Hong Kong • Seoul • Taipei • New Delhi
Cape Town • Madrid • Mexico City • Amsterdam • Munich • Paris • Milan

PEARSON EDUCATION LIMITED

Edinburgh Gate
Harlow CM20 2JE
Tel: +44 (0)1279 623623
Fax: +44 (0)1279 431059
Website: www.pearsoned.co.uk

First published in Great Britain in 2007

ISBN: 978-0-273-70868-1

British Library Cataloguing-in-Publication Data
A catalogue record for this book is available from the British Library

Library of Congress Cataloging-in-Publication Data
A catalog record for this book is available from the Library of Congress

10 9 8 7 6 5 4 2
10 09 08 07

Typeset in Scala 10.5 on 15 by 25
Printed and bound in Great Britain by Henry Ling Limited, at the Dorset Press, Dorchester, DT1 1HD

The publisher's policy is to use paper manufactured from sustainable forests.

Contents

List of figures   viii

Foreword   xi

Acknowledgements   xv

Introduction   xix

1 The power of dreams   1

Mission control   2
The vision thing   3
The plan   4
Beyond strategic planning   4
SWOTs need not apply   9
From planning to dream-making   10
Redefining the future   13
Summary   15

2 House of dreams   17

Building the house   17
Shooting for the moon   20
The pillars of achievement   21
Building on solid foundations   22
House rules   23
Whose house?   26
One house or many?   27
The multibusiness context   28
The House Model challenge   31
When a single page is not enough   32
Reality checking   37

Grounding the dream   39
When dreams become nightmares   41
Summary   44

3 Jump-starting the dream   **46**

Short is sharp   46
Preparing to dream   47
External perspectives   48
Internal perceptions   59
Proof reading   61
The dream ticket   62
CEO as householder   67
Summary   68

4 Sharing the dream   **73**

Day-dream believers   74
Back it or sack it   76
Selling the dream   81
Gotta luv it   85
Great expectations   88
Insomniacs need not apply   89
Keeping the dream alive   90
Summary   91

5 Living the dream   **94**

Personal discipline   96
Corporate semaphore   97
Corporate discipline   105
The house that Jack built   106
The umbrella approach   109
Staying in touch   110
... and following through   113
Turning ideas into action   113
Summary   114

6 Built to dream ... with open eyes   **116**

Supporting the vision   116
The dream team   120
Role casting   122
All together now   124
How big?   126
First principles   129
Taking appropriate measures   131

Plots and plans 132
Meaningful metrics 134
Rewarding what matters 135
The devil is in the behavior 136
The power of no 137
Just doing my job 139
Every dogma has its day 141
Summary 144

7 Dreaming on ... with open eyes 146

The four cornerstones of continous execution 149
Discipline 149
Trust 151
Support 153
Stre-e-e-t-c-h 154
Linking the four 156
Built to be different 157
Summary 160

Conclusion: just dream it 163

Early warning systems 163
In a nutshell 165

List of figures

Figure 1.1 The difference between classical planning and
creating dreams with a deadline   10

Figure 2.1 The House Model   18
Figure 2.2 President John F. Kennedy's 'Man on the moon'
address, 25 May 1961   19
Figure 2.3 Martin Luther King, Lincoln Memorial,
Washington, DC, 28 August 1963   20
Figure 2.4 Vision Express' vision   21
Figure 2.5 Synchronicity and congruence of the vision   26
Figure 2.6 The link between corporate and business
unit visions   28
Figure 2.7 Trucks and cars   29
Figure 2.8 Cars in Europe   30
Figure 2.9 From vision to letter of intent to story   41

Figure 3.1 Constructing scenarios   48
Figure 3.2 Using your most challenging scenario as
a backdrop   49
Figure 3.3 Expanding into other industries from mobile
phones   51
Figure 3.4 Combining different inputs for customer insight   61
Figure 3.5 Suggested schedule for a two-day workshop   63

Figure 4.1   A dream with a precondition   81
Figure 4.2   Cascading the vision   82

Figure 5.1   Symbols and signals as a means of focusing   96
Figure 5.2   The different manifestations of signals and symbols   102
Figure 5.3   Initiatives   107

Figure 6.1   AXA's marketing structure up to 2005   118
Figure 6.2   AXA's revised organizational structure, focusing on
              customer segments rather than products   119
Figure 6.3   The size of the corporate center depends on the
              strategy chosen   127
Figure 6.4   Coordination mechanisms depend on the degree
              of centralization   129
Figure 6.5   The vision plan   133
Figure 6.6   The Pareto principle reversed   142

Figure 7.1   The difference between trust and support in
              terms of execution power   151
Figure 7.2   The four elements of continuous execution   156

Foreword

Over the years, no business process has more successfully embedded itself into the lexicon of organizations large and small than *strategic planning*. For decades, the *gravitas* surrounding the creation of a company's strategy has put the process on a pedestal above all other activities. The literature, much of it authored by celebrated icons of business theory, abounds with endless exploration of the concept, from how-to models to organizational philosophy. So, every year, like pilgrims to a shrine, executives and their staffs, from CEOs to financial and marketing heads, throw themselves into the ritual of creating, documenting, and adjusting their organization's Strategic Plan.

But unfortunately, the technical vocabulary of those plans – the *market shares*, the *ROICs*, the *risks and vulnerabilities*, and the like – often stands in the way of the very outcome they hope to achieve. Caught up in the detail, well-meaning executives lose sight of the beacon, and like a sailor in shifting seas, often find themselves well off course. Moreover, too many strategic plans defy all efforts made to communicate them out to the real points of execution – the larger employee base. Operating with only a vague sense of the real meaning of the organization's strategy, it is never clear to employees whether each of their incremental decisions are in support of the plan, or contrary to it. Thus, despite all of the time, effort and resources put into its development, the strategy usually fails to inspire the employee and connect him or her in any real way to the goals of the organization. The result is bad execution and, often, organizational failure.

Well before the birth of all of the theories behind modern strategic planning, there were successful, break-though companies and business models. In every aspect of life there were products and services that revolutionized life as we knew it before, and there were companies delivering those products and services and, along the way, creating value for their investors. Those successes often had their roots in the simple dream or aspiration of the company's founder. And those dreams were stated in the simplest of common language, understandable by all who heard them. The tasks necessary to fulfill the dream were generally few and clear. They were accompanied by equally straightforward 'rules of the road', outlining behaviors in support of the underlying dream. Usually by necessity, those dreams had *real* deadlines associated with them subject to the founder's financial wherewithal. They attracted like-minded people who executed the tasks with a loyalty born in an understanding of, and agreement with, the higher purpose.

Walt Disney was one of those dreamers. In creating the first Disneyland in California, U.S.A., he was fulfilling his own simple dream of creating 'some kind of entertainment deal where parents and the children could have fun together'. From that simple dream came a family entertainment empire that today spans the globe, hosting over 100 million visitors per year. His dream revolutionized family vacationing in America and elsewhere around the word, and continues to serve as the guiding principle for the creation of new Disney entertainment.

While close to my heart, Walt Disney was not alone in espousing and executing simply stated dreams. Henry Ford, Pierre Omidyar, Bill Gates, and Adi Dassler, to name a few, all figured out how to reduce their strategic goals to the simplest of statements, understandable to this day, even without any knowledge of the prevailing business environments in which they were made. And each created consumer and investor value of astounding significance.

But how does one do this in today's complex, ongoing organizations set in a rapidly changing business environment? This book provides keen insight into the answer to that very question. In order to avoid the potential trap of an overly complicated strategic planning process with unsatisfying results, forget all the jargon and figure out your *dream* for your organization, and when you'd like to achieve that dream. The remaining building blocks necessary to insure that the entire organization embraces your dream and is your ally in making it a reality are detailed in ways that make sense, are actionable and will inspire a different way of thinking about how to go about making real change in your organization.

Dream with the passion of a company founder!

James A, (Jay) Rasulo
Chairman, Walt Disney Parks and Resorts Worldwide
November 13, 2006

Acknowledgements

I would like to thank my clients, those companies that were willing to experiment a different way of deciding on their future, companies that chose to be unique, companies that made the choice of energizing their organizations, generating enthusiasm and commitment through a shared vision of the future.

I would like to thank my former colleague at IMD, Pierre Casse, with whom I ran the first visioning exercises.

My thanks also go to IMD, which gave me the time and space to write this book.

Finally, I would like to thank all of the PED participants for their willingness to be stretched, to generate visions even before they went back to their companies. Their enthusiasm led to over 500 visions being created over the course of three years. Their involvement in the visioning process, the requirement that they convince an entire class of executives that the dream was worth living, participated in the soundness of the model.

Thank you.
Jacques
May 2006

A book is a very special project to work on. Crystallizing ideas, turning experience into shared knowledge, and combining action and theory in a way that others may find useful is both challenging and fun. My thanks therefore go first to Jacques for giving me the opportunity of working on this project with him. They also go to IMD, for providing a unique place that encourages constant learning and growth in a truly international environment. A special word of thanks for those faculty members who were willing to serve as mentors and teachers, sharing experience and knowledge openly, providing support, encouraging stretch, and showing trust, while trying to keep my eclectic interests focused! Des Dearlove and Liz Gooster provided invaluable editorial feedback, and Estelle Jaquier always provided the missing link, with a smile.

Our opportunities in life are also determined by what our parents have gifted us. A special thought to my father, for his gift of intellectual curiosity, and to my mother, for her gift of creativity and passion. And to the three men in my life: Ake, Christopher and Alexander, for the gift of love.

Anne-Valérie
May 2006

Publisher's acknowledgements

We are grateful to the following for permission to reproduce copyright material:

Adidas AG for the 1998 brand mission statement (this has since been revised and updated); AXA for information presented in Figures 6.1 and 6.2.

Message to Congress, 25 May 1961, John F. Kennedy

First, I believe that this nation should commit itself to achieving the goal, before this decade is out, of landing a man on the moon and returning him safely to the earth. No single space project in this period will be more impressive to mankind, or more important for the long-range exploration of space; and none will be so difficult or expensive to accomplish. We propose to accelerate the development of the appropriate lunar space craft. We propose to develop alternate liquid and solid fuel boosters, much larger than any now being developed, until certain which is superior.

We propose additional funds for other engine development and for unmanned explorations – explorations which are particularly important for one purpose which this nation will never overlook: the survival of the man who first makes this daring flight. But in a very real sense, it will not be one man going to the moon – if we make this judgment affirmatively, it will be an entire nation. For all of us must work to put him there.

Let it be clear – and this is a judgment which the Members of the Congress must finally make – let it be clear that I am asking the Congress and the country to accept a firm commitment to a new course of action – a course which will last for many years and carry very heavy costs: 531 million dollars in fiscal 1962 – an estimated seven to nine billion dollars additional over the next five years. If we are to go only half way, or reduce our sights in the face of difficulty, in my judgment is that it would be better not to go at all.

Now this is a choice which this country must make, and I am confident that under the leadership of the Space Committees of the Congress, and the Appropriating Committees, that you will consider the matter carefully.

It is a most important decision that we make as a nation. But all of you have lived through the last four years and have seen the significance of space and the adventures in space, and no one can predict with certainty what the ultimate meaning will be of mastery of space.

I believe we should go to the moon. But I think every citizen of this country as well as the Members of the Congress should consider the matter carefully in making their judgment, to which we have given attention over many weeks and months, because it is a heavy burden, and there is no sense in agreeing or desiring that the United States take an affirmative position in outer space, unless we are prepared to do the work and bear the burdens to make it successful. If we are not, we should decide today and this year.

This decision demands a major national commitment of scientific and technical manpower, material and facilities, and the possibility of their diversion from other important activities where they are already thinly spread. It means a degree of dedication, organization and discipline which have not always characterized our research and development efforts. It means we cannot afford undue work stoppages, inflated costs of material or talent, wasteful interagency rivalries, or a high turnover of key personnel.

New objectives and new money cannot solve these problems. They could in fact, aggravate them further – unless every scientist, every engineer, every serviceman, every technician, contractor, and civil servant gives his personal pledge that this nation will move forward, with the full speed of freedom, in the exciting adventure of space.

Speech at the Lincoln Memorial, Washington D.C., 28 August 1963, Martin Luther King

Let us not wallow in the valley of despair, I say to you today, my friends.

And so even though we face the difficulties of today and tomorrow, I still have a dream. It is a dream deeply rooted in the American dream.

I have a dream that one day this nation will rise up and live out the true meaning of its creed: 'We hold these truths to be self-evident, that all men are created equal.'

I have a dream that one day on the red hills of Georgia, the sons of former slaves and the sons of former slave owners will be able to sit down together at the table of brotherhood.

I have a dream that one day even the state of Mississippi, a state sweltering with the heat of injustice, sweltering with the heat of oppression, will be transformed into an oasis of freedom and justice.

I have a dream that my four little children will one day live in a nation where they will not be judged by the color of their skin but by the content of their character.

I have a *dream* today!

I have a dream that one day, down in Alabama, with its vicious racists, with its governor having his lips dripping with the words of 'interposition' and 'nullification' – one day right there in Alabama little black boys and black girls will be able to join hands with little white boys and white girls as sisters and brothers.

I have a *dream* today!

Introduction

A dream: *an ideal, aspiration, or ambition.*
(OXFORD ENGLISH DICTIONARY)

Forget strategic planning. What every organization needs today is an inspirational vision of the future – a dream. But it cannot be an open-ended dream. It must have a beginning

what is needed is a dream with a deadline

and an end: in short, what is needed is a dream with a deadline. This book tells you how to create the future vision of you company. It is written for all those who care about what the future holds for them and for their organization. It is a book for dreamers, but dreamers with the courage and commitment to make their dreams come true.

Every company has, at some point in time, crafted a blueprint of where it wants to go and how. Typically, the entrepreneur will look at their environment and decide that there is something that is not being done, or could be done better. They then create a business to meet that need. That need is the mission. The entrepreneur doesn't know where the business will be in three or five years' time; they just know that there is something that can be improved on. As they launch the business, they start working backwards from the future, creating a vision.

A vision is the next step for a business. It is forward-looking – or at least it should be. But the most common way of designing that vision, and working towards achieving it, is by using a strategy formulation process that is backward-looking. The big problem with the way most organizations create their future plans is that they extrapolate from the past, using a strategic planning method that starts with today, looks back at yesterday and uses the information to determine what the company will be doing tomorrow.

Depending on the culture of the company and the preferences of the senior team, the strategic planning will be detailed or broad. In the detailed approach, strategy formulation is the result of a full-fledged analysis of the company, its environment, its competitors, suppliers and clients, typically involving several consulting firms and running for hundreds of pages. The downside? The more clearly defined the strategy, the more strongly it becomes set in stone, the harder it is to change when change is needed.

Alternatively, the corporate strategy is something as vague as 'diversify into complementary business segments'. Without specifying what that means, the company ends up wasting resources and losing itself in a portfolio of unrelated businesses, with no clear reason for existing. This is the 'broad brush' approach, and a lot of companies fall into this trap. Swissair, Switzerland's national airline for 71 years, pursued its ill-fated 'hunter strategy' on the advice of McKinsey and Company. The idea was that Swissair should acquire or gain majority control of any airline it could, at almost any cost. The airline collapsed in 2002.

In addition, it is very difficult to obtain support and coordination from staff in an organization that is too loosely coupled. No-one knows or agrees on what the company's priorities should be, leading to chaos, fiefdoms and disengagement. The result is rarely helpful, and sometimes it is disastrous. The trouble with looking over your shoulder the whole time is that, even if you take tiny steps, you can still walk straight over the edge of a cliff – many companies have done just that.

The central premise of this book is that the way companies decide their future has to change. Strategic planning no longer works – if it ever really did. When the road to your future becomes so detailed that there is no room to seize new opportunities, then it is bound to fail. If it takes so long to design that by the time the plan is announced the environment has shifted, it will generate high levels of frustration and disengagement both for those who worked on the plan and for those on whom it is imposed. The result? Major strategic decisions are taken outside the plan, and those having to implement the plan resent the fact that they were not consulted upfront.

Most important of all, perhaps: the world does not stand still long enough for such a process to work. Today's business environment is moving too fast to be sufficiently understood by those who design the strategy. Companies are increasingly spread out across the globe, with centers of competence and innovation far removed from headquarters. As a result, any blueprint must be a much more collaborative effort, involving key decision makers from large subsidiaries, important markets and functions.

today's business environment is moving too fast to be sufficiently understood by those who design strategy

It is for all these reasons and more, that we advocate replacing strategic planning with a vision, or dream. It is better to have a short vision that is filled in as events unfold, than a strategic plan that cannot know ahead of time what the opportunities and changes will be. If you don't believe this, just look at what happened to the ultimate case study in central planning, the Soviet Union. Its Five Year Plans were largely works of fiction. The Soviet empire eventually fractured under the weight of its own moribund planning system.

Likewise, the traditional strategy planning process of corporations no longer works – if it ever did. Business leaders can no longer survive and be successful without taking the entire organization with them, without sharing a common vision that generates enthusiasm, commitment and energy.

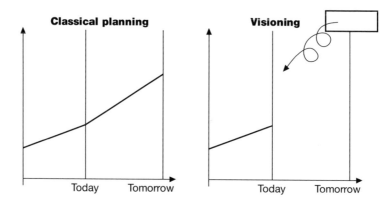

The vision: a process to create the future rather than forecasting from the past and present

1 The power of dreams

If people relate to the company they work for, if they form an emotional tie to it and buy into its dreams, they will pour their heart into making it better. HOWARD SCHULTZ, CEO, STARBUCKS [1]

In the early 1990s, an Italian wine grower named Moretti Polegato attended a wine industry conference in Reno, Nevada. A keen jogger, he packed his running shoes. Every day after the conference, he went for his daily run. But in the stifling Nevada heat, he suffered in his rubber-soled shoes. Polegato was a resourceful individual. He decided to cut holes in his outsoles to let in some air. It worked. Back in Italy, he designed a prototype for a shoe that breathed – his new design let heat out without letting water in. Polegato then approached a number of established shoemaking companies with the prototype. No-one was interested. At this point the idea might have died. But Moretti Polegato was a determined man. More than that, he had a dream. So in 1998 he founded Geox to market his own product. Today, the company is Italy's leading and the world's third-ranking footwear brand, with revenues of €455 million for 2005.

Such is the power of dreams in business.

Or think of Amazon, the on-line bookstore founded by Jeff Bezos in 1994. A former investment banker, Bezos had two motivations – he was annoyed that his wife could not find a publisher for her work, and he was fed up with waiting in line in book stores. By its fourth month of existence, the company was selling more than 100 books a day. In 1996, its first full fiscal year in business, Amazon generated

US$15.7 million sales – a figure that would increase by 800 per cent the following year. While the stock rose and fell over the next few years, today the company is a solid investment, and Bezos' philosophy has not

the better you can make your customer experience ... the more customers you'll attract

changed: 'The better you can make your customer experience ... the more customers you'll attract, the larger share of that household's purchases you will attract. You can become a bigger part of a customer's life by just simply doing a better job for them. It's a very, very simple-minded approach.' And it has nothing to do with a SWOT analysis. This forces us to reflect on what it takes to be successful in an industry and whether past experience is still an indicator of future success.

What links these two very different companies is a vision – a dream of what they wanted to achieve. In this chapter we look at why companies need a vision; what makes a good vision; and why the traditional ways of determining a company's future are no longer up to the job. But first we need to understand the difference between vision, mission and strategy-making. These are three tools that help companies decide on the future, but they are often confused. While there are many different definitions of these terms, below are our definitions.

Mission control

The mission defines boundaries, and explains why you are in business. It is an overarching principle that rarely changes. It serves as a general guideline, but it does not tell you what your next step should be.

The mission, then, is the answer to the question: 'What business am I in and for what purpose?' It is the thread that links all the visions together so that they tell a story. For example, 3M's mission states that its business is to solve unsolved problems innovatively. This will not change over time, although its visions will. Below are a few examples of mission statements.

Solve unsolved problems innovatively (*3M*)

Make technical contributions for the advancement and welfare of humanity (*Hewlett-Packard*)

Experience the emotion of competition, winning and crushing competitors (*Nike*)

Give ordinary folk the chance to buy the same things as rich people (*Wal-Mart*)

The vision thing

The second tool is the vision. Leaders need a vision. Without one, an organization or even an entire nation can appear to be adrift. When asked about his longer-term view, for example, George Bush Senior, while President of the United States, famously fluffed his response, dismissing it as 'oh, the vision thing'. Bush never managed to shake off his reputation as a short-term thinker.

The vision is what enables us to define the future, to work towards a specific objective. It changes over time – once you have achieved one objective, you move on to the next.

the vision is what enables us to define the future, to work towards a specific objective

Today, multinationals across the world proudly display a vision and mission statement on the first page of their annual reports. The current trend is to have one per business, and to include something about sustainable growth and corporate social responsibility. However, all too often these vision statements lose their meaning and their ability to take a company and its people into the future in a focused and realistic way. Here are some examples of typical vision statements:

A PC on every desk (1987) (*Microsoft*)

Democratize the automobile (early 1900s) (*Ford*)

Become the Nike of the cycling industry (1986) (*Giro*)

We will destroy Yamaha (1970s) (*Honda*)

Become number one or number two in every market we serve and revolutionize this company to have the strengths of a big company combined with the leanness and agility of a small company (1980s) (*GE*)

The examples demonstrate several things. First, that there is often confusion between vision and mission. Second, many vision and mission statements are interchangeable – they are not unique to the company that designed them. Third, most of these statements do not include a time-frame, which takes away a certain concreteness and sense of urgency.

The plan

This brings us to strategic planning – the third tool organizations use for deciding on the future. Strategic planning is how you plan to reach your vision. Almost every company uses a strategy planning process. Unfortunately, this is often just an extrapolation from the past, generating very little enthusiasm or innovation. In this sense, many companies have substituted a strategy process for a vision. Let's be clear: the vision comes first; strategic planning is how you get there.

In this book we will focus primarily on visions and how to execute them. Why? Because a mission does not tell you how to get there and strategy formulation does not generate the energy and commitment you will need to succeed, which is the basic problem with how most organizations go about deciding their future. Typically, they use the strategic planning process to generate the vision – rather than the other way round. Think about it. A set of directions are no use if you haven't decided where you want to go. Yet, most companies devote a huge amount of time, money and energy to this task.

Beyond strategic planning

In most large organizations, the strategic planning process is akin to some primitive tribal ritual. As Eric Beinhocker and Sarah Kaplan note in the *McKinsey Quarterly*: 'There is a lot of dancing, waving of feathers and beating of drums. No-one is exactly sure why we do it, but there is an almost mystical hope that something good will come out of it.'[2]

In reality, very few senior executives believe that the process of strategic planning serves a useful purpose. The outcome is seen as the result of heavy corporate politics around resource allocation and power, yielding very few new ideas.

For many years, the classical schools of strategy held sway (see Figure 1.1 for some definitions), influencing how companies viewed their business and their environment, and above all, dictating how they defined their position in their industry. While they have provided invaluable tools and helped formulate winning strategies, we believe that, for a number of reasons, these ideas (listed below) are inadequate when dealing with the challenges faced by companies today. (See Table 1.1 for a quick reference.)

Table 1.1 Problems with traditional strategy formulation

Stability is an illusion: too time consuming and too lengthy to develop

Risk aversion is risky: too incremental and too much of the same

Planning is too far from the action: crafted in isolation from the field

Intuition is blinded by analysis: does not allow for new perspectives

Compliance is not commitment: no shared perspective of the future

Management is not leadership: not a leadership tool

Stability is an illusion

First, the traditional approach works on an assumption that the environment is sufficiently stable that what is formulated remains valid for implementation. Unfortunately, the world is no longer like that – if it ever was. Take the Danish dairy company Arla. When a cartoon that it had no part in creating was published in a local newspaper it had no control over, the company's entire business in the Middle East was wiped out in the course of a month.[3] Through no fault of its own, Arla's products were boycotted following protests against Denmark and Danish companies. Arla lost 10 per cent of its revenue overnight (K400 million).

strategy must be created quickly

It is an extreme case, perhaps, but it illustrates the point that strategy must be created quickly. You can spend six months on a beautiful report, but by the time you are done, it will be probably already be out of date – the world will have moved on.

Risk aversion is risky

The second issue is that the traditional strategy process is inherently risk averse. It is geared towards taking a small, incremental step from the previous year (and all the years before that). Typically, this involves as little risk-taking as possible. No-one wants to raise their head above the parapet. The primary purpose of the strategic planning exercise becomes matching resources with a given environment, and as a result the tool neither helps in dealing with uncertainty nor encourages creative thinking. The danger is that the organization walks over the edge of a cliff one small step at a time. It fails to energize employees and it certainly does not encourage them to share a dream around a common future.

Any strategic decision that departs from the past involves a certain risk – a leap into the unknown, a new experiment. So there is no way of knowing ahead of time whether an existing competence will prove to be a strength or a weakness. When Nokia moved from televisions and rubber products into mobile phones at the beginning of the 1990s, it

in periods of high uncertainty, risk does not lie in not having a strategy but in having one that was cast in stone too early

made a leap in the dark. There was little it could do to assess whether the competencies that had served it in its previous business would be of use in its next venture. In periods of high uncertainty, risk does not lie in not having a strategy but in having one that was cast in stone too early. The strategy then serves as blinkers, blocking peripheral vision.

Planning is too far from the action

A third problem is that associated with distance. It is similar to what could be found in traditional military hierarchy: the people in the back row – crafting the strategy – are far removed from the soldiers on the front who can do nothing other than implement the strategy, even if it is ill-fitted to what they can see is happening in the field. The strategy is formulated in isolation, in an ivory tower often six or seven levels removed from reality, the result being that the final product is often ill-suited to the constantly shifting reality.

Intuition is blinded by analysis

The managers who work on strategic planning often come from strong analytical backgrounds. And yet, as we mentioned, Amazon could never have been started using analytical strategic planning. Particularly in the youth of an industry, you have to use intuition rather than analysis. Many breakthrough companies were not started by people who knew their environment by heart, but rather by newcomers who came in with a new perspective and were often snubbed by the 'establishment'. Think of Geox, the Italian shoe company discussed at the start of this chapter.

Compliance is not commitment

Forcing a strategy top-down results in compliance rather than commitment from those charged with its execution. In a business context with high uncertainty, however, you need more than compliance – you need excitement and commitment. The enthusiasm generated by a shared perspective of the future should draw people into feeling committed to supporting the company's vision. Sitting down and saying 'let's do this together' not only generates this much-needed commitment, but also helps make a company more resilient when undergoing change. Ownership – a shared and committed view on the future – means that everyone is on board to make it happen. It means your employees take the initiative and work beyond their assigned job description. It means that everyone looks at how to improve what already exists, working out ways to reach the common objective. You can see from Table 1.2 below how commitment and compliance differ and why commitment is more helpful.

Table 1.2 Compliance and commitment compared

Compliance	Commitment
Do when asked	Do because you are convinced
Do only what asked	Do new things when reality does not fit
Never modify what is asked, even if it doesn't work	Do well, do the utmost, to make sure that it works

Management is not leadership

Finally, in the traditional approach you simply roll out a detailed action plan that describes resource allocations, budgets and financial targets. This approach fails to take into consideration the distinction between managing and leading. Yet this distinction is critical – managing is about optimizing what you have while leading is going forward in a certain direction. Resource optimization is hardly an effective way of taking people with you. At the opposite end, leading is about people and the ability to generate the excitement and commitment we believe are essential elements of successful execution.

SWOTs need not apply

To close this discussion, we would like a word with that traditional strategy technique, the SWOT analysis (Strengths, Weaknesses, Opportunities and Threats). In 1997, Hill and Westbrook[4] surveyed 50 UK-based companies, looking at their strategy-making process. They found that 20 of these used some form of SWOT analysis (with the help of 14 – yes, 14 – different consulting companies). They also found that none of these companies subsequently used the results of the SWOT analysis.

This is a serious problem – the analysis consumes a lot of time with very little result. The ensuing business plan often has no connection to the analysis, reinforcing the feeling of divide between the plan and the action. But the greater issue with the approach is that for every opportunity you can find a threat; for every strength you can find a weakness. What you consider a threat or opportunity depends on where you stand. Can you really know your strengths and weaknesses before acting? One could argue that competencies are not necessarily distinctive to an organization but also to its context, the situation and the way in which they are used. For example, a supermarket chain may find that fast food restaurants are closer to its business competencies than discount stores because the core competence in both businesses is the ability to move perishable goods through an efficient chain of distribution.[5]

> **for every opportunity you can find a threat; for every strength you can find a weakness**

When Howard Schultz, the CEO of Starbucks, says, 'For my part, I saw Starbucks not for what it was, but for what it could be. It had immediately captivated me with its combination of passion and authenticity', he is not talking about the result of a SWOT analysis. Instead, he talks of passion and authenticity – the language of personal commitment, of enthusiasm, of energy. These are the powerful components of a different way of deciding on the future.[6]

All of these points lead us to believe that the classical models of formulating strategy fail. We move now to suggesting a different approach to deciding on your future. The difference can be summarized using the diagram shown in Figure 1.1.

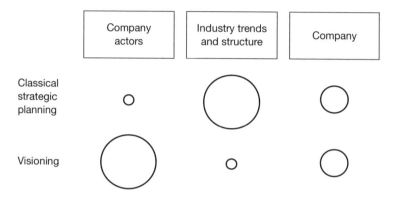

Figure 1.1 The difference between classical planning and creating dreams with a deadline

From planning to dream-making

The main problem with the classical approach to strategy-making is its inability to deal with turbulent, complex, rapidly changing – often unpredictable – environments. The muddled and complicated process that results in endless pages of analysis and recommendations blurs the simplicity of the questions that the plan must answer. The agility and flexibility required of organizations today means you need to generate energy and not lose yourself in details, and the resulting vision must be more than a beautifully crafted statement. It must be inspiring.

the resulting vision must be more than a beautifully crafted statement. It must be inspiring

The future is about answering some simple questions:

1 What business or businesses should we be in – and with what competitive advantages?

2 How do we get there? Should we create Greenfield operations, partnerships, acquisitions, licensing? And by when?

Answering these questions is the first step in the process that will help formulate the company's vision in a way that is both exciting and sustainable.

Some companies do have visions that convey a dream. These are written in such a way that employees can identify with them and understand where the company wants to go; they are exciting, sustainable and both ambitiously and concretely inspirational. The most famous of these is probably Microsoft's 'A PC on every desk in every home', while others include:

Ford will democratize the automobile (*Ford Motor Company* (early 1900s))

Become the company most known for changing the worldwide poor quality image of Japanese products (*Sony* (early 1950's))

Become the dominant player in commercial aircraft and bring the world into the jet age (*Boeing* (1950))

Become a $125 billion company by the year 2000 (*Wal-Mart* (1990))

The points we have made above about the flaws in the existing strategy formulation process can be combined with our definition of a vision as a dream with a deadline, to express what we believe makes a good vision. Such a vision – or dream – has a number of characteristics. It must:

Inspire with ambition. A good vision should be short and inspiring. The best visions are short because then everyone can remember them, and they are inspiring through the language that they use, for example 'Ford will democratize the automobile'. Everyone can remember and relate to that vision.

Be achievable. There is no point in saying that you will be the number one company in the world in two years from now if you are a small start-up operation. For example, one of the authors (Jacques) is the founder of a company called 'Châteauform', a European-based corporate venue provider. When the company decided to expand its operations from its original location north of Paris, it did not try to expand all over Europe, but stated as a first step (or first dream) 'Let's encircle Paris'. This vision was ambitious – it called for the acquisition of several more castles around Paris that could be turned into seminar venues – but it was not unrealistic.

Inspire with realism. A good vision should reflect the degree of urgency best suited to the organization's situation. A short timeline may not be very inspiring if the company is not going through a crisis. Similarly, if the

> **a good vision should reflect the degree of urgency best suited to the organization's situation**

urgency is felt by all to be high, it is no good suggesting a ten-year deadline. In fact, there are situations were a vision should not/cannot be expressed, for example when the company is in crisis and the urgency is so great that tomorrow may not exist. In other situations you may want to create a sense of urgency in a relatively stable environment as a means of supporting change and generating energy. The deadline is not as much about the actual urgency, as it is about what those who will follow you will be able to believe.

Be measurable. You must be able to know when you have reached your objective. Wal-Mart's 'Become a $125 billion company by the year 2000' is clearly measurable. Other goals are not that easy to measure in financial terms, but we will be looking at the many ways in which success can be measured.

Have milestones. The vision should specify what it takes to get there in the form of actions and milestones, and should be clear on how progress will be measured, success recognized and rewarded. It should also state how to stay in touch with reality and get back on track if needed.

Be shared by everyone in the organization. When everyone is committed to the same objective alignment comes easily. One of the best ways of sharing a vision is to have a story which people can relate to and be inspired by. Euro Disney's 'Lets' win the hearts of Europe' speaks to people's emotions and to the need to win. It is inspiring in a positive way. Their vision brought the company back on track, turning profits a year earlier than had been projected. Kennedy's speech about putting a man on the moon was a story – a story that appealed to people's dreams as explorers, as achievers. Furthermore, it called for commitment, while providing focus and a specific timeline 'before the end of the decade'. Kennedy's dream became reality in 1969, when Neil Armstrong set foot on the moon and returned safely.

We would even argue that it is more important to have a vision that is shared than a vision that is right.

Redefining the future

In short, we believe that the need for simplicity, agility and inspiration calls for a new way of defining the future. It calls for companies to replace strategic planning with a vision –

the need for simplicity, agility and inspiration calls for a new way of defining the future

and not just any old vision. It must be a vision that provides the inspiration of a dream. We define a vision as a dream with a deadline. This definition conveys not only the energy, commitment and enthusiasm that we believe are necessary components of a good vision; it also forces the essential time dimension. Let's be clear, there is no point in dreaming if there is no deadline. An open-ended dream runs the risk of becoming a hallucination.

In Chapter 2, we will show you how two famous visions work – Kennedy's, and that of Martin Luther King – through a tool we call the 'House Model'. This simple one-page framework encompasses all the building blocks of a good vision: the dream, how to get there and the supporting behaviors. In Chapter 3, we explain how you can use the House Model to create your own dream with a deadline.

There are a number of advantages to building a vision on a single page, of which the principal one is the fact that you have nowhere to hide – there is no blinding with science – no endless pages of statistics and no analysis. Executives seem to find it much harder to fill in a single page than they do to fill 300. If you can't define the future of your company on a single page, that page remains empty, and if the definition of a plan is to 'make a decision today for tomorrow', then you have failed. The one-page model forces those designing it to think about tomorrow. Other advantages to the House Model include the facts that it:

- ❖ forces those building it to focus on the key points
- ❖ makes for a holistic rather than an analytical plan
- ❖ avoids the issue of people tuning out beyond the first page
- ❖ is inclusive – there are no independent areas.

A vision, or dream, is only as good as its execution, which is why in Chapter 4 we explain how you can share the dream to ensure the commitment of everyone in your organization. Then in Chapter 5 we examine the discipline needed to live the dream and make it a reality. Chapter 6 looks at the structures that an organization must put in place to support its vision of the future, while Chapter 7 looks at the four cornerstones of execution.

All of these chapters refer back to the House Model.

In essence, this is a book based on a model that combines both formulation and execution. We then build on this model to look at some of the hurdles to executing visions and provide hands-on, practical tools to help you achieve your dream. For example, if your next dream is to 'create the safest and most exciting car experience for modern families' (Volvo) you will probably need a very different organization and set of values from those required if your goal is 'to give ordinary folk the chance to buy the same thing as rich people' (Wal-Mart). Your method of organization and your focus will be very different.

The model we champion in this book makes certain assumptions about the quality of those who will be in charge of execution. You will need charismatic leaders, or at least leaders who can help others share the dream, taking them into the future, which is why we insist that the model is a leadership and not a management tool. The road into the future is not described step-by-step, which means that you will need leaders who can bring people on board while creating alignment and focus. In short, you will need leaders who are prepared to lead from the front.

Summary

A vision helps a company decide on its future. But the traditional way of deciding on the future is flawed in several ways:

- ❖ The process is so time-consuming that by the time a strategy is established it is obsolete.
- ❖ Strategies are crafted with such precision that they leave no room for opportunity.
- ❖ They are designed far from the front-line.
- ❖ They are often the result of analysis rather than intuition.
- ❖ They are a management rather than a leadership tool.

These flaws mean that visions generated through traditional strategy-formulation fail in their role to provide focus and alignment towards achieving a common goal. Their inability to generate enthusiasm and commitment hinders the execution process.

Our approach is very different.

- ❖ Rather than working incrementally towards a future determined by the past, we suggest working with a realistic, time-bound dream, which can come from a variety of sources. It is only once the dream has been defined that the gap between the dream and today can be assessed and bridged.
- ❖ This process of coming up with a dream with a deadline is supported by the House Model, a one-page framework encompassing all the building blocks of a good vision: the dream, how to get there and the supporting behaviors. The

approach combines both formulation and execution, looking at some of the hurdles to executing visions and providing hands-on, practical tools to help you execute.

❖ A good vision must generate commitment and enthusiasm. The vision should be short, inspiring, measurable and achievable. It should clearly outline how the company intends to reach its objective, while leaving room to seize opportunities as they appear. It must be shared, and it must reflect the adequate degree of urgency.

But you might ask: is it enough to provide the sense of direction that a dream offers? Based on our research and experience, the answer is a resounding yes. Whether you take John F. Kennedy's dream put forward in 1961 and achieved in 1969, or Bill Gates' dream of a computer on every desk running Microsoft, providing direction and encouraging innovation is the best way to create the future.

providing direction and encouraging innovation is the best way to create the future

NOTES TO CHAPTER 1

1   Howard Schultz (1997). *Pour Your Heart Into It*, Hyperion, 6.

2   Eric D. Beinhocker, and Sarah Kaplan (2002). Tired of strategic planning?, *McKinsey Quarterly*. Special edition, 49–57.

3   Cartoons associating terrorism and Islam (and in particular vilifying Prophet Mohammed) appeared in the Danish press in October 2005. These were picked up by Islamic organizations a few months later, leading to large scale unrest as both sides fought (freedom of press versus respect for religious beliefs), until the global scale of the response involved ambassadors from many countries, the United Nations and international boycotts.

4   T. Hill and Roy Westbrook (1997). SWOT analysis: It's time for a product recall. *Long Range Planning*. 30(1), 46–53.

5   Henry Mintzberg and JamesWaters (1982). Tracking strategy in an entrepreneurial firm, *Academy of Management Journal*, 25(1), 465.

6   Schultz (1997), 4.

2 House of dreams

We were always pushing boundaries beyond where
our industry's conventional wisdom suggested we could go.

BERNIE MARCUS AND ARTHUR BLANK (HOME DEPOT) [1]

In this chapter we look at the different building blocks that combine to create a vision that is both inspiring and concrete. We will dive straight into what we call the House Model, looking at the three components of a good vision: the dream (the roof), the key ways (the pillars) and the supporting behaviors (the foundations).

Thinking about creating your vision using the House template is a powerful way to keep the process simple. It also forces all those involved to think the vision through so that it can be crystallized on a single page. This means making choices and selecting only those actions and behaviors that are critical to reaching the set objectives.

The House Model is best completed using a short, intensive, team effort, in the form of a workshop, bringing together the key decision-makers, and including a cross-section of the different businesses and functions. Chapter 3 will consider the design and content of this workshop.

Building the house

There is a sequence to the formulation of the vision, which can be represented in a schematic drawing of a house, starting with the roof, followed by the pillars and the foundation. First you decide where you want to go (the roof), then you decide how you will get there (the pillars) and then you make sure that you are on solid ground (the foundations). Together, the roof, pillars and foundations tell a story that is unique to the company (see Figure 2.1).

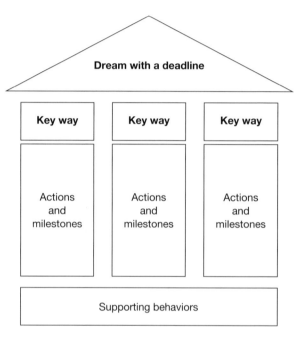

Figure 2.1 The House Model

The model has one key advantage over the traditional way of deciding on the future: by going beyond the words in the vision to describe actions, milestones and desired behaviors, the vision becomes concrete, and the ensuing plan can be implemented. In addition, the deadline makes it real, conveying urgency. When your vision is something like 'We will be No. 1 in our industry', you may have followers, even believers, but what you really want is

by going beyond the words in the vision to describe actions, milestones and desired behaviors, the vision becomes concrete

believers who can take action because that action has been defined and a time-frame determined. This can be illustrated going back to Kennedy's speech and slotting the different elements of his speech into the model, as shown in Figure 2.2.

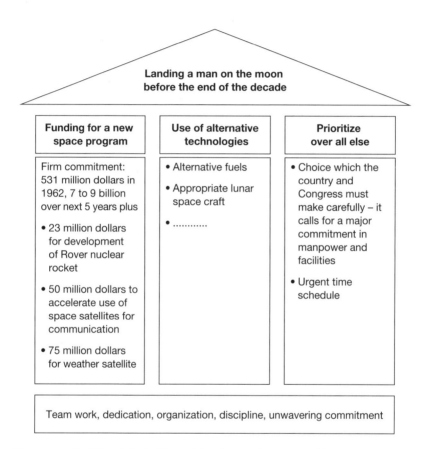

Figure 2.2 President John F. Kennedy's 'Man on the moon' address, 25 May 1961

Similarly, Martin Luther King's famous 'I have a dream' speech can be represented on the House Model as in Figure 2.3.

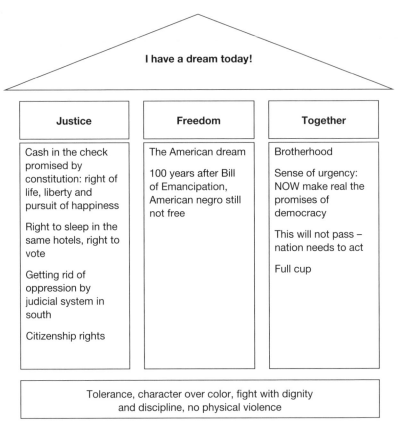

Figure 2.3 Martin Luther King, Lincoln Memorial, Washington, DC,
28 August 1963

Shooting for the moon

The roof of the house is the dream with the deadline. It should be a single sentence. In 1998 Vision Express, a UK-based optical services store reformulated its vision to 'become the best store in town by 2007'. The company recognized that while its 'one-hour' optician concept spurred growth, the company rated worst in class for the quality of its customer service and the design of its stores. The new vision was ambitious yet achievable. Terence Conran's CD team was hired to redesign the stores, and important resources were put behind finding the best location in each city. Since then, other designers have been hired to create visually arresting stores. The company grew successfully to own 200 stores all over the UK. The vision was achieved and the company achieved its objective of having the best stores (irrespective of type of business) in each location.

The pillars of achievement

The pillars spell out how you will achieve your vision, outlining the corporate or competitive advantage defined in Chapter 1 as simple questions that help shape the future. The titles of the pillars (key ways) describe the source of competitive advantage. For instance, going back to our Vision Express example, the key ways would include 'best

Figure 2.4 Vision Express' vision

location', 'best teams' and 'best customer service' (see Figure 2.4). These key ways were benchmarked not only against other optical stores but against every other store in town. The body of the pillars are a bullet-point list of the actions that must take place for the vision to happen – for example, under 'Best stores', actions and milestones might include 'buy stores on the high street', 'spend x on redesign per year' and so on. To achieve that action, the company must agree on what price it is willing to pay to obtain better locations and better stores. It needs to decide how it will reward its employees to create the best teams. Or how many stores it wants to open per year. The actions and milestones include elements from all the functions in the organization, giving everyone a voice, thereby increasing the level of engagement and commitment.

All the action points in the pillars must be measurable (if not quantifiable). For example, there is only a yes/no answer to the question 'Have you launched the induction program?' (set as an objective in the pillars). And the point is not to look for scapegoats – if the program was not launched, for whatever reason, then a new date has to be agreed on. Measurement does not have to be direct – it can be through proxy variables, such as articles in the press, customer feedback, patents registered per year and so on. We will be looking at measurement in more detail in Chapter 5.

Before we proceed any further we should perhaps explain why we chose to have three pillars in the house model, as opposed to four or more: research has shown that most people can remember a maximum of four things easily, but find it difficult to remember more than four. So three pillars (and three key ways) plus a dream make a total of four things to remember.

Building on solid foundations

The foundations represent the supporting behaviors. Behaviors are the concrete representation of the values: words like 'team spirit' or 'honesty' remain vague; whereas 'everyone is responsible for what happens in the store' sets clear limits and sends a strong signal as to what is acceptable or not, and what each individual's responsibility is. For example, Starbucks is well known for how well it treats its staff. This is demonstrated through concrete actions such as a health-care program that includes part-timers and stock ownership for all employees. Schultz argues that people connect to Starbucks because they relate to what the company stands for – respect, trust, the feeling of community that is translated by the baristas as they tell you about your coffee. The values have successfully been translated into behaviors that make the coffee shops and the company attractive to its customers as well as to its employees.

As we saw in Chapter 1, you will not find it easy to fill in a single page when for years you have filled in many pages. Having to design something short tends to make you numb. Yet this is the best way of crystallizing your thinking, making choices and determining actions. Remember that this is about deciding on the future of the company and on how to close the gap between the dream for tomorrow and the reality of today.

this is about deciding how to close the gap between the dream for tomorrow and the reality of today

House rules

As you fill in the different building blocks of your vision, ask yourself the following questions:

Is your one-line vision, your dream:

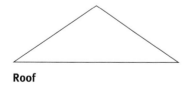

Roof

Inspiring?

A stretch, yet achievable?

Is it written in clear and simple language that everyone can understand?

Short (less than ten words)?

Measurable?

To keep it simple, do not mention in the dream what business you are in. This is an internal document and people should know.

Your key ways:

Key ways

Do the titles accurately describe the sources of competitive advantage (or comparative advantage) for a multi-business company?

Is there a logical and obvious link with the dream?

If we do all of these well, can we succeed? (Do we have the right three key ways?)

Are they short? (Less than five words to keep it short and to the point.)

Do they read as a story together with the roof? (As with the example above: best stores, best locations, best customer service.)

Your action points and milestones:

Pillars

Are the actions well spread over the 3–5-year period between now and when the dream should come true? (i.e. not everything this year.)

Are the action points and milestones measurable? (Yes – no – number – proxy.)

Are the key activities of the company's business system represented?

Is there an obvious link with the key ways?

Are they short – each less than ten words?

Are all the columns evenly filled in? (It's not easy to simplify in three columns and then find the same number of actions for each key way.)

Are they at similar levels of generality/detail? ('Hire one new person' is not the same as 'build five new factories'.)

And finally, with behaviors:

Foundations

Are the chosen behaviors measurable?

Do they help achieve the key ways?
If these behaviors are not present, what will *not* happen? (Dream, key ways, priorities.)

Have we limited ourselves to a maximum of five behaviors?

Do they relate easily to our company values?

With these questions in mind, refer to Figure 2.5 and see if you can fill in the model for your company. It is important that all the different parts of the vision are consistent with one another. Thinking of the roof and the key ways as a story helps maintain consistency.

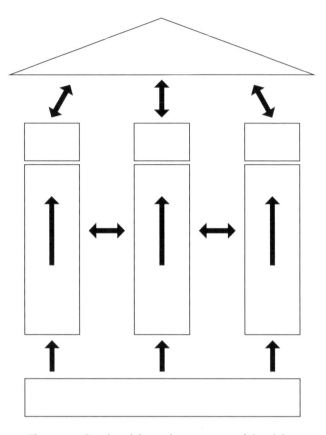

Figure 2.5 Synchronicity and congruence of the vision

Whose house?

The house must be designed by the people responsible for its execution. At the business unit level, this would be the executive committee and those who report to the executive committee. As we will see in Chapter 3, within reason, the bigger the team the better for sharing, and ideally, the board should participate in the formulation.

it is the result of a consultation between the different functions, encouraging commitment and participative efforts

The house must be the result of a collective effort – one of its primary characteristics is that it is the result of a consultation between the different functions, encouraging commitment and participative efforts. As such, it calls for each individual to play two roles: a functional one (marketing, finance, etc.) and one as a corporate citizen, taking into consideration the company as a whole.

This approach has several advantages over the classical approach. First, because the vision cuts across locations, functions and hierarchical levels, and the entire organization is represented, encouraging the feeling of having been consulted and therefore creating a greater desire to participate. Second because a greater number of people are involved, the vision is easier to implement. Both points mean that the sharing or espousing of the vision is greater.

One house or many?

There are two types of business contexts in which visions need to be developed. The first is the single sector, single industry, single business context. In this case, a single vision (and therefore only one house) is needed. The other is the multibusiness context, where the industries are unrelated and therefore so are the businesses (for example General Electric's businesses range from financial services to power systems).

For a multibusiness company there are two levels at which the vision can be developed: the business unit level and the corporate level. The corporate vision may be seen as a unifying concept that defines the key competence of the group, across the different businesses. The corporate-wide vision addresses comparative advantage while the business unit visions address competitive advantage. The guiding principle is that the vision developed must make sense for the company as a whole, be it corporate or business-unit specific. You may choose to develop regional or even country-specific visions if the situation **the vision developed must make sense for the company as a whole, be it corporate or business-unit specific** calls for this level of differentiation. But you should always ask yourself whether the exercise adds to your competitive advantage or not. The link between the two is illustrated in Figure 2.6.

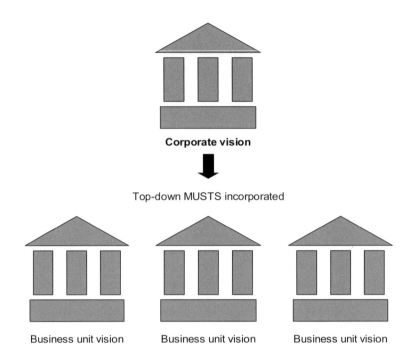

Corporate vision

Top-down MUSTS incorporated

Business unit vision   Business unit vision   Business unit vision

Figure 2.6 The link between corporate and business unit visions

The multibusiness context

In addition, the company needs to ask itself 'What makes us, as a group, better for our shareholders than if they owned shares in an individual company?' It needs to be clear what makes it better for a company to act as a single entity. This is the question analysts continually ask of conglomerates such as General Electric or Vivendi Universal.

Corporate advantage has essentially to do with three dimensions:

❖ *Risk* – the company does better than an individual investor at adding and subtracting businesses from its portfolio.

❖ *Synergy* – economies of scale.

❖ The *allocation of resources* – financing operations. The allocation of resources has to do with the willingness to finance operations that an individual shareholder would find too risky or a bank would not consider part of its mission.

A company normally has a degree of speed, scope and power in taking those actions that is greater than that of a single individual.

Consistency is equally important at this level: whatever you do vision-wise at the business unit level has to be consistent with what is being done at the corporate level. Consistency is generated by pursuing the same focus and objectives across the organization, which in turn creates synchronicity.

Achieving synchronicity means that the different parts of the business have to meet, talk and negotiate. Different business units will naturally come up with business plans that have different priorities: for

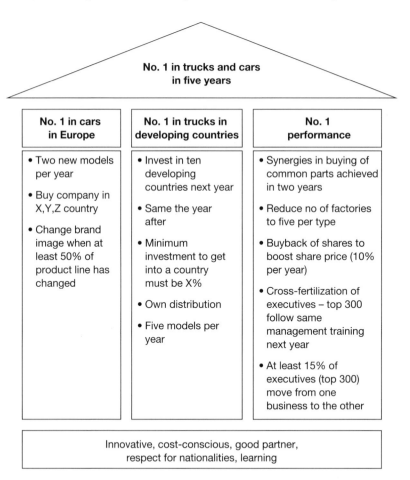

Figure 2.7 **Trucks and cars**

one it may be the acquisition of a business, for another it may be to build a new plant. Compromises will have to be made.

Let us take a simple, hypothetical example. An automotive company decides that it wants to become the No. 1 transportation company in Europe by 2011. To achieve this vision, the company decides to prioritize selling cars to developed countries, and trucks to developing ones. The businesses are therefore separate, with separate priorities. But the divisions need to agree on which models will be developed, and work together to generate economies of scale (for example through common platforms and common purchasing). This will only happen if there are clear guidelines coming from the top. In our model synchronicity translates into the 'top-down MUSTS', which we will discuss in detail in Chapter 3. Figures 2.7 and 2.8 show an example of what the House Model for the automotive company would look like, first at the corporate level and then at the business level.

Figure 2.8 Cars in Europe

The House Model challenge

The House Model, despite its apparent simplicity, is a challenging exercise in several ways:

* **The need to be selective.** It is much harder for an executive group to fill one page than 300, because it forces them to be selective with their choices. The House Model forces all those involved to think about what is crucial to achieving the dream. Every word in the key ways and milestones has to help implement the vision. Every behavior has to support the vision.

* **The need for consistency.** The need for consistency requires the business take a holistic view. It is more than just adding together a number of business plans – it is about designing common strategies that together lead to the execution of the vision.

* **The need for focus.** This is about identifying milestones that lead to accomplishing the vision and ignoring anything that distracts from that objective. It is about being selective.

* **The need to involve the entire organization.** The House Model is inclusive and cuts across all of the functions, businesses and countries in the organization. For the model to be successful, the organization has to come together and work as one in the pursuit of a common dream.

* **The need to work back from a projected point in the future.** The vision as we define it is a dream that you work back from, looking at what it will take to

> **the vision as we define it is a dream that you work back from**

close the gap between where you want to be and where you are. This is much more difficult to do than to add incrementally year after year.

* **The need for every milestone and action to be measurable.** This approach demands that everything be measurable, be it by direct measures (financial metrics) or by indirect measures that we call proxies – indicators that by themselves do not tell the story but

together tend to indicate that you are going in the right direction (for example newspaper articles and customer satisfaction surveys).

❖ **The need for simplicity**. The House Model is more difficult to complete as a strategy exercise because you do not have the excuse of being able to get lost in details. Those completing the exercise must know clearly where they want to take the company. A list of incremental actions will never generate the excitement and energy that a dream will.

When a single page is not enough

Some companies cannot conceive of a vision on a single page. Below we discuss a three- to four-page alternative. The two versions fulfill different purposes but can be used together. Both are self-contained documents. Let us look at the example of adidas, below.[2] As you will see from the example below, each important word is clearly explained, laying out in plain terms what the company wants to achieve and where it is going; adidas uses the word mission in its documentation, but this is clearly a vision.

BEING THE BEST

adidas is dedicated to becoming

The Best Sports Brand In The World[1]

The Brand Mission Statement, which relates to all products and services bearing the brand marks, contains four key words: 'best', 'sports', 'brand', and 'world'. There is a need for everyone at adidas to understand what these terms mean and to relate this mission statement to our daily activities, from finance to sales, design to development, marketing to advertising, distribution to customer service. But most

1 The examples in this box are taken from 1998, and the company structure and brand mission statements have since evolved.

importantly, to understand what this mission means to the world of sports, our teams, our events, and our athletes.

Being the best

Being the best means exceeding all others in our industry. This does not necessarily mean being the biggest. Our goal is to have our consumer and the industry believe that a real athlete wears adidas to reach peak performance. If we are the best, then size will follow. We will know we are the best when real athletes in all our major categories choose adidas footwear to help them achieve peak performance. Being the 'best' means:

- Excelling all others in *Performance*. Shoes and apparel should be designed and manufactured to *be used in the* sport for which they were intended.

- Excelling all others in *Technology and new Product Development*.

- Excelling all others in *Design*. Adi Dassler said an athlete must look and feel good in his 'equipment' in order to perform at his best. Therefore, adidas must continue to lead in design and use of colors.

- Excelling all others in *Quality*.

- Excelling all others in *Customer Satisfaction*.

- Excelling all others in *Value*.

- Excelling all others in *Communicating* – both internally and in the marketplace.

- Excelling all others in the quality of our *People* and the opportunities available to them.

We cannot look to industry rankings to see whether we are the best. We will know that we are the best when we are respected.

The Meaning of 'Sports'

By sports, we mean the physical participation in competitive activity. It's the body in motion, it's blood-racing, heart-pounding action. It's the challenge of individual against individual, team against team. It's not thinking about it, talking about it, watching it or hanging on the fringes.

'Sports' should not be limited to traditional organized or team activities. New sports are always emerging and evolving. adidas should be an essential part of these sports.

Our brand strategy is to be associated with any activity that is *Physical* and *Competitive*.

- 'Physical' is the *activity* of sport, not reflecting upon it.

- 'Physical' is the equipment of sport versus the fashion of sport.

- 'Physical' is the body in motion.

- 'Physical' is blood-racing, heart-pounding action.

- 'Physical' means participating in sport.

- 'Physical' is the difference between the playing field and luxury box seats.

- 'Physical' is the locker room versus the press room.

Being 'competitive' means challenging another or oneself. To compete means that some boundary must be crossed – manifested by the athlete against himself, the athlete against others, or the athlete against his or her physical environment. In other words:

- 'Competitive' is attacking a mountain top.

- 'Competitive' is attacking the last hurdle after 400 m.

- 'Competitive' is attacking a record.

- 'Competitive' is commitment to being prepared to compete.

In short, if it is not physical and competitive, it is not sport. And if it is not sport, it cannot be representative of the adidas brand.

The brand

A product is not a brand.

A product has only physical attributes, while a brand is a broader, more nebulous concept. It is a collection of perceptions about a product, formed by personal experience or by various types of communication, which define its identity and personality. The brand image described by these perceptions exceeds the life of the product and, if positive, adds value, reassurance and differentiation beyond the merely functional.

For adidas to be the best, it must develop a brand – products and image – which earns the respect of everyone. And, everything that everyone does in the company must do justice to the brand, recognizing how difficult it is to build and how easy it is to destroy.

The adidas brand must not appear on or be associated with any product or activity that does not have its roots in a physical or competitive activity. If we are not advancing the brand, or positioning the brand to move into a potential sport business, or placing the brand in a market where it might otherwise not be, but where it belongs, then the adidas marks should not be used.

The world

adidas is a global brand with European roots, yet with a single mission. This is not to say that we do not have our regional differences. Nor does it mean that we cannot be flexible to enable us to react to changing needs, markets or cultural differences. What it means is that we must have a unified vision of what we do, why we do it, and who we do it for. To be the best in the world, adidas must be the brand of choice in every market.

To successfully market the brand worldwide, we must first accept a few basic truths about global marketing in today's world:

● The overriding principle must be that all marketing (global, regional or local) must support or enhance the position and direction of the brand.

● All marketing is global – whether it is seen or unseen, for good or for ill, it has impact.

● All elements of a marketing plan must be locally relevant advertising, public relations programs, promotions, and in-store displays work from one country to the next, or from one region to the next, only if they make sense to the consumers. This cannot be used as an excuse to only do local activities – the brand comes first.

● Communications make sense from culture to culture, from country to country, only if they focus on the similarities among the consumers being targeted.

The consumers adidas is targeting are athletes. These consumers care about their sports. They care about performance. They are physical. They are competitive. They expect the best ... from themselves and their athletic products. This is not different anywhere in the world. This is our core message ... and the message must be the same anywhere in the world. If it is not the same, it is not adidas.

By focusing on athletes, we also meet the needs of a larger group of consumers who want sport-inspired products. In other words, sport is the vehicle to get to the street – if it is right for the athlete, it will be right for the consumer.

What our brand stands for does not vary ... that is global. Now the message is conveyed may vary. Think of the athletes' village at the Olympic Games – everyone is different, but they all share a common vision and common goal.

In both the one-page and three-page versions of the model, the process by which the vision is created is the same. Only the format of the output is different. The primary difference is that once you have come up with your dream you explain what you mean for each word, using one page per word. The three-pager may be particularly useful in some situations, for example for new businesses. Below are the key differences between the two versions (see Table 2.1).

❖ The three-page version is strong on the intentions, but weaker on the horizon. In the three-page version you spend more time explaining the vision as opposed to translating the vision into concrete actions and milestones. You may want to use it as a brief for the company (this is what we do and don't do in this company), and add to it to make it more concrete (letter of intent, individual objectives and so on).

❖ The three-pager is a good communications tool. Some companies use the three-page version as a brief for advertising agencies. The House Model cannot be used for this purpose – it is a strategic document strictly for internal use.

❖ The three-page version gives the different business units more freedom in choosing their course of action.

Table 2.1 The advantages of the one-page model and the three-page model

One-page (House Model)	Three-page
A single snapshot	Can *explain* the meaning of each important word for everyone
Sharp with visual bullet points	Easier link to brand positioning in the marketplace
Easier to measure	Serves for briefing in all institutional communication about the company
Tracking of progress is straightforward	Can be transformed into a book of standards for different functions, for example new product introduction

Below is Bata's summarized three-page vision. As you can see, the team spelt out the important words of the vision to describe what the company was about and where it wanted to go.

Bata's vision: Closest friend in the world for your everyday fashion footwear and more

❖ 'Closest friend' – a strong word – being the closest friend means excelling in understanding and addressing LOCAL consumer needs, and building a strong relationship with them.

❖ 'In the world' means leveraging product development, sourcing, back-room processes and best practices to bring the best possible choice, design and value to local customers.

❖ 'Everyday fashion footwear' means contemporary styles, comfortable from dawn to night and trendy, so that the product is not a commodity.

❖ 'And more' is about providing a level of product and service that goes beyond just footwear.

Source: Company documents.

In the original document, each word is explained on a single page. To make it more concrete Bata added action points and milestones to the key elements. For example, to become a client's closest friend, you need a high level of staff retention. This means investing in staff through training and incentives. It also means creating an 'easy-to-shop' environment, where the client feels at ease. This in turn requires that you offer something beyond just price, and provide your client with a positive shopping experience.

Reality checking

For all our talk of dreams, the vision cannot, must not, be a hallucination built to feed the personal egos of a top team. A number of

the vision must not be a hallucination built to feed the personal egos of a top team

warning signals can help you determine whether your vision has
derailed:

- ❖ You have no followers. This might be because the vision was not
  sufficiently well explained, or was under- or over-ambitious. In
  either of these cases, people do not think it will happen, will not
  put any effort into making it happen and may even ignore it.
- ❖ You are not walking your talk. For example, your key ways state
  that customer relations are important, but you fail to train your
  employees in good customer service and you do not try to keep
  your employees long-term.
- ❖ You have confused the vision with an advertising slogan and the
  exercise is void of any meaningful content.
- ❖ You do not review it every year, looking at achievements and
  adding new milestones and actions for the following year.

The elements that go into the design of your vision are based on an
existing reality – in fact, one of the most important inputs in the two-
day seminar is the question 'What have we done well and what haven't
we done so well?' Using these factual inputs you build an intellectual
construct that becomes your dream.

There is one risk that must be avoided at all costs – that of becoming
dogmatic – of saying 'We have this vision, we won't change any of it,
and no matter what, we will continue with it, even if we don't see any
results.'

There are a number of reality checks that can avoid this from happening. One of these is to ask questions, and ask them both internally and
externally, for instance, 'Are we making progress?' 'Do our customers
see it?' Your customer is a fantastic judge
because their view is unbiased. If you are
hesitating between two options, they probably
know what they would have liked, and this is the
need that you want to address. In parallel, you
should check with all the departments/functions – front-line operations
(which are particularly important in large companies where you may sit

**your customer is a
fantastic judge
because his view is
unbiased**

seven or eight hierarchical levels away from your sales team), R&D, and marketing. If you have designed a strong set of key performance indicators, they will tell you the story of your business and how it is evolving.

Reality checks consist of taking your different sources of reality and matching them to the pillars and milestones in your vision. Using the gaps, look for patterns of why the vision is not happening. At Euro Disney they ran a management forum every second month. Members included the executive committee, and the two levels below them (a total of about 350 people). At every meeting, questions were asked and answered and results analyzed to align the company further toward its vision of winning the hearts of Europe. Once the key issues had been identified, there was a follow-up. However good you think your vision is, you must consistently confront it with the reality of a fast-changing world, in which your competitors are not static players on the chess board.

Beyond these warning signals, it is critical to link resource allocation to the vision – it is this link that turns the vision into something concrete. In our model this is done through the letter of intent.

Grounding the dream

The link between the vision as depicted in the House Model and the annual allocation of resources is the *letter of intent* (see Table 2.2). Ideally this letter should be a single page, and a maximum of two. The

Table 2.2 Letter of intent

Date of completion:	
Main thrust for the year:	
Actions (as a list)1, 2	
Musts and shoulds	
Financial objectives	

title should spell out the main thrust for the coming year, and the content should include concrete, specific action points, 'musts' and 'shoulds', as well as the financial objective. We recommend that you draft one letter of intent per year.

In 2004, Châteauform's vision was 'Be number one in Europe five years from now'. The letter of intent for the first of these five years therefore looked at preparing the company for growth. The main thrust of the letter was 'Preparing our company for internationalization' and the actions included hiring local managers in the target countries, ensuring that the senior management team spoke several languages, and so on. The following year, when Châteauform was ready for international expansion, it once again broke down its vision into a new small step in its letter of intent: 'Let's attack southern Europe'. Together, the letters of intent tell the story of how you achieved your vision.

letters of intent tell the story of how you achieved your vision

You should share the letter of intent with your team, getting commitment on the actions. The team should have the freedom to push back on the actions and objectives. The letter will serve as the basis for budgeting. The consistency between the vision and the letter of intent means that you avoid the typical frustration of suggesting a budget that is turned down because it is deemed 'not in synch with the vision'.

Once the letter of intent has been agreed on, your next step is to determine individual objectives that will support the intentions. These are part of the normal objective-setting process for each employee.

The time between the development of the vision and the creation of the letter of intent depends on the normal planning cycle. We would suggest that you select carefully when you do your visioning exercise so that the gap between the two is as small as possible.

All of this together builds a very tight, integrated process – from the dream all the way down to individual objectives (see Figure 2.9). The steps are clearly laid out: we create a vision, we format it, we share it. After that we look at the implications for actions, including the budget and the individual objectives. A major part of the success in implementing the vision resides in the tightness of the process (summarized in Figure 2.9).

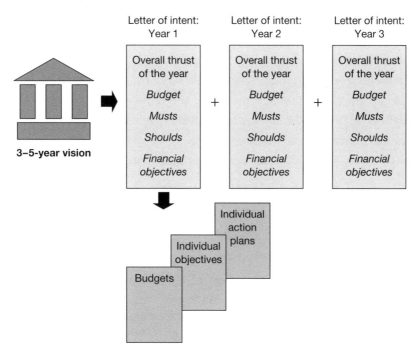

Figure 2.9 From vision to letter of intent to story

When dreams become nightmares

The story of Vivendi Universal's rise and fall is an illustration of what goes wrong when a CEO loses his focus and tries to go too fast, grow too big and maybe become too unreal (the hallucination versus the dream) as he implements his vision.

Transformation of the company: Messier's first era

In 1996, Jean-Marie Messier, former civil servant and investment banker, took over as chairman and CEO of Companie Générale des Eaux. The French water and sewerage utility founded in 1853 under Napoleon III had turned into a giant conglomerate encompassing real estate, healthcare and telecommunications. Under the former CEO,

Guy Dejouany's, leadership, core businesses went from representing 80 per cent of revenue to 46 per cent and the number of subsidiaries increased from 280 in 1976 to 2,714 in 1996. The group employed 217,000 people. By 1995, however, it was in deep financial trouble, having spread its resources too thinly and suffering from the crash of the real estate market. Immediately, Messier worked on refocusing the company on its core activities, identified as:

- ❖ utilities (water, waste, energy and transport)
- ❖ communications (telecommunications and multimedia)
- ❖ construction and property.

These he divided into two categories – the businesses of today (utilities and construction) and the businesses of tomorrow (communications). While Messier believed the future of the company lay in communications, he could not reduce the importance of utilities and property immediately – water, while representing only a quarter of sales, represented 80 per cent of CGE operating profit.

On his mission to rejuvenate the company, Messier focused on profitability rather than volume – he dismantled most of the 2,700 subsidiaries and reduced direct reports from over 70 to a dozen. He insisted that the entire company focus on the creation of shareholder value. In addition, he built a coherent corporate structure, with clear reporting lines and policies for resource allocation. (Previously the heads of subsidiaries had been able to start and acquire businesses and did so extensively; there was no formal asset allocation system.) For the first time, the company actually had an organizational chart. Finally, Messier designed a performance-based management incentive system linking the largest businesses to return on investment targets.

All these measures generated investor confidence, and by the end of 1997, the stock had appreciated by 72 per cent.

So far, so good. Then the second phase began.

Media mania?

In line with Messier's belief that the future of the company was in communications, the company's mission was redefined as 'To become the world's preferred creator and provider of personalized information, entertainment and services to consumers anywhere, at any time, and across all distribution platforms and devices'. Messier stated that the company's ambition was 'To be the world market leader in the five fields of content that we consider as key for this digital age: music, movies, games, education and sport'. In 1997, Messier acquired Havas and changed the company name to Vivendi, a name that was to represent the new orientation and culture of the company and unite the different businesses. In 2000, the company bought its first major operation in the US, acquiring Seagram, the Canadian liquor group which owned Universal. The name was changed accordingly, to Vivendi Universal. By 2001, Messier had transformed the company into the world's second largest media group. He had morphed from someone bent on focus and rationalization into a deal-maker.

In July 2002, Jean-Marie Messier was ousted from his role at the head of Vivendi and replaced by Rene Fourtou. That year, the company posted France's biggest-ever annual corporate loss: €23.3 billion. The previous year, the loss had been €13.6 billion, due mainly to the collapse in the value of the acquisitions – basically, many of the companies purchased had been overpriced, and Vivendi had paid these excessive prices in their desire to create an integrated global media company. Analysing the rise and fall of Vivendi, analysts point to a series of mistakes committed over a very short time-frame: he over-promised, over-paid, over-rushed, unglued and under-explained where he was taking the company. In short, first the dream developed into a hallucination, and then it ended in a nightmare.

Summary

The House Model is a simple, schematic way of representing all the key elements that go into the design of a good vision.

- ❖ The roof of the house is the dream with a deadline.
- ❖ The pillars represent how the dream is to be achieved, including action points and milestones.
- ❖ The foundation represents the supporting behaviors.

We have looked at the type of questions you can ask to determine whether you have a solid House Model or not.

It is important to decide upfront who will develop the schematic of the house, agreeing that at the very least it should involve the senior executive committee. The fact that the House Model is the result of a collaborative effort is one of its strengths, which is why, should the corporation need to develop both corporate and business unit level visions, it needs to make sure that these visions are consistent and synchronous, building on one another and supporting the overall vision of the company.

the fact that the House Model is the result of a collaborative effort is one of its strengths

Naturally, even the most simple of models has challenges. The House Model is no exception. In our case they include:

- ❖ the need for focus and consistency
- ❖ the need to involve the entire organization
- ❖ the need to work back from a projected point in the future
- ❖ the need for every milestone and action to be measurable
- ❖ the need for simplicity.

For those who cannot imagine working an entire vision into a single page we suggest the three-page alternative. This option, while being more explicit in its description of the vision, serves more as a communications tool than a strategic document.

Finally, we considered some of the warning signals that the vision has derailed, including not walking one's talk, having no followers, confusing a vision with an advertising slogan and omitting to review the vision versus the progress made (on a yearly basis). We also made the link between the design of the vision and the allocation of resources through the letter of intent.

NOTES TO CHAPTER 2

1 Bernie Marcus, Arther Blank and Bob Andelman (1999). *Built from Scratch: How a Couple of Regular Guys Grew the Home Depot from Nothing to $30 Billion*. Crown Business.

2 Jacques Horovitz, Giana Boissonnas and Ursula Hilliard (1998) adidas (b). IMD case study. IMD-3-0744.

3 Jump-starting the dream

Whatever you can do, or dream you can do, begin it.
Boldness has genius, power, and magic in it.

WILLIAM HUTCHINSON MURRAY (1911–1996)[1]

In this chapter we discuss the process by which the vision, or dream, is defined. While the previous chapter was about outputs – what makes for a good vision and the different elements that need to be included in a good vision – this chapter looks at how to get there – the process of formulating the vision. We start by looking at the tools and methods that are used to provide a variety of inputs for the vision, after which we will discuss who should participate and why the participation of the CEO is essential to the success of the process.

Short is sharp

a good vision can be developed within a very short time-frame

Contrary to commonly held belief, a good vision can be developed within a very short time-frame. In fact, the shorter the time-frame, the more those participating in its formulation will remain focused and enthusiastic.

We suggest jump-starting the visioning process with a two-day workshop, involving anything from 5 to 100 participants. The first day is a day in which information is shared and created together, and the second day is one in which the vision is agreed on and a strategy for sharing it across the organization developed.

In order for the visioning process to be successful, good preparation is essential. This preparation is both intellectual and organizational. The intellectual preparation happens through the inputs, the organizational preparation through the flash survey, both of which we will look at below.

Preparing to dream

There are a variety of inputs that can help us think differently about our business and our environment, and assess where we stand as a company compared to where we want to go. We suggest focusing on the following types of inputs, grouped into three categories:

❖ **Perspectives** (the external world)
 — Inputs to revisit the boundaries of your business and its environment.
 — Inputs to challenge your perception of customer trends.
 — Inputs to challenge your business model.

❖ **Perceptions** (internal to the company)
 — Inputs through the flash survey (employee perceptions).

❖ **Proofs** (facts about the company)
 — Inputs on where you stand as a company.

Table 3.1 Perspectives, proofs, perceptions

External world	Facts about the company	Internal world
Industry boundaries	Past successes	Employee feedback
Trends	Past failures	Flash survey
Business model	Past performance	
Perspectives	Proofs	Perceptions

Information on all three categories should be assembled before you come to the seminar. This information will then be presented and discussed in the course of the first day (which we call the input day). Below we look at each type of input in detail.

External perspectives

This group of inputs focuses on the external world. What are the mega-trends that are shaping your environment and creating new markets? What does your customer research suggest? This type of input is best obtained by looking at trend reports, observing customer behavior, new competitors and new offerings.

A well-known method of coming up with new ways of looking at your business is through scenarios. This method was pioneered by Shell in the 1970s and is now widely used. Variants include asking questions about extreme situations in the future, for example 'What will you do if oil reserves run out?' 'What if consumers stop drinking coffee for health reasons?' 'What will you do if your cigarettes are outlawed?' Figures 3.1 and 3.2 present a model which you may want to use as a way of creating scenarios and choosing among different potential futures.[2]

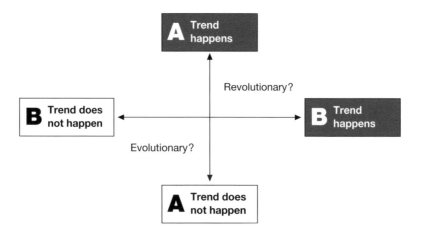

(i)   Position players in terms of existing business models
(ii)   Discuss how the main trends will develop over time
(iii)   Select the two most critical uncertainties
(iv)   Pick one or more of the resulting quadrants as scenario settings
(v)   Incorporate the established trends to 'flesh-out' the scenarios
(vi)   Give each scenario an evocative title

Figure 3.1 Constructing scenarios

Using your most challenging scenario as a backdrop

a) How will the scenario affect customers, in terms of their buying criteria, new product development and the growth of markets?
What part of your business is converging?
What part of your business is diverging?

b) Which of the players in the vertical industry chain will benefit most from the scenario?
Which player is likely to gain bargaining power and make the most money?
How is the balance shifting?

c) How will competitors change their behavior to deal with the scenario? (How will they appeal to a customer segment? How will they manage the business activity system? How would you summarize the viable competitive strategies?)

d) What kind of players are most likely to win?

Figure 3.2 Using your most challenging scenario as a backdrop

Another way of generating input is to take your top team to places that will encourage them to think differently by providing an unusual environment – a desert, a mountain trek, working with a conservation project. Hindustan Lever, for example, sends all of its new recruits to villages in the Indian countryside, to help them understand who their customers really are. There is no reason why this should not also happen at the senior level. Another trend is for large companies to hold board meetings in India, helping the board assess the potential of the market. Nokia, HSBC and ARM Holdings all held board meeting on the subcontinent last year.[3]

Pushing the industry boundaries

Revisiting and redefining the boundaries of the industry to uncover new opportunities is a powerful way of rethinking your business. Doing this means not accepting the role that you hold in a certain industry, nor the limitations of that industry.

There are many famous examples of companies that have success-fully redefined the boundaries of their business. Companies such as Nike and adidas successfully moved from the traditional sports shoe industry into sportswear before moving further into casual and street-wear – they expanded from their core, evolving and tapping into new markets. And this doesn't happen only in the consumer industry – Danfoss, the Danish manufacturer of electronic and mechanical heating and cooling devices, redefined one of its businesses from being a supplier of automatic air filters to being a 'technology leader in all products related to clean air'.[4] Along the way they rewrote their mission statement – 'making modern living possible'.[5] SKF Bearings went from being a provider of ball bearings to offering 'trouble-free operations for factory managers with machinery'. This redefinition enabled them to move into the field of preventive maintenance: replacement of bear-ings, dust management, lubrication and machinery use.

IMD, the international business school based out of Lausanne, Switzerland, underwent a similar redefinition of its executive education business. The school's mission is now 'accompanying multinational corporations in their strategic adaptation'. Custom-made programs for corporate clients represent over 50 per cent of the school's activities (workshops, one-week seminars), a clear shift from when public, open-enrollment programs represented the majority of the programs of clas-sical business schools. This shift came with clear boundary changes – the faculty went from being educators to facilitators, and programs moved from being transactions to becoming workshops with pre-program work and post-program follow-up.

Another well-publicized redefinition of boundaries is the mobile phone industry, with hand-held devices offering an increasing number of functions ranging from cameras to personal assistants, computers and MP3 players. Figure 3.3 shows the different industries that converge under the new mobile phones.

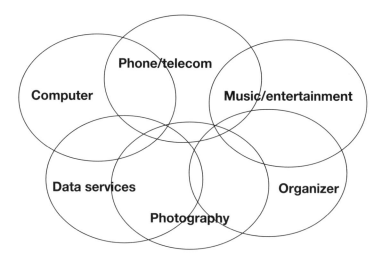

Figure 3.3 Expanding into other industries from mobile phones

Challenging customer trends

Challenging the existing perceptions in an industry is difficult. There is a certain arrogance, an 'it has always been this way' 'this is what people want' attitude that is difficult to confront, especially when there may not be any real sense of urgency. Looking at consumer trends is a refreshing way of understanding what consumers and customers really want. Volvo asked its customers the same question it was asking internally: 'What do we want for the worldwide future?' The answers were primarily around safety, around cars for large families but also about design. The result became part of the company's vision and mission statement:

> **looking at consumer trends is a refreshing way of understanding what consumers and customers really want**

> **OUR VISION:** TO BE THE WORLD'S MOST DESIRED AND SUCCESSFUL PREMIUM CAR BRAND.
> **OUR MISSION:** TO CREATE THE SAFEST AND MOST EXCITING CAR EXPERIENCE FOR MODERN FAMILIES.
>
> *Source:* Volvo website: www.volvo.com.

At first glance, working on trends is simple – you need to answer two questions: what's in? What's out? For example, caviar houses, cigars, home redesign are all in. And what's out? Retail banks, classic supermarkets ... But understanding mega-trends goes beyond a quick analysis of one's competitors and partners, simply because they may also have missed the trend. Let us look at some examples of mega-trends and how these might affect business.

One of the most publicized and undisputable mega-trends of the early twenty-first century is the aging population of baby boomers in the Western world, and the corresponding shift in what this population wants.

The baby boomers are the generation born between 1946 and 1966. They are the wealthiest and most influential generation ever. Baby boomers represent approximately 17 per cent of the population in industrialized countries today, and will represent about 25 per cent of that same population by 2015. In Japan, this 'silver generation' owns half of Japan's US$11.3 trillion in savings, and spends US$95 billion a year on new products, home care and home renovation. In the United States there will be 120 million 'golden oldies'[6] by 2025, representing two-thirds of the country's wealth. These aging baby-boomers represent a huge potential for marketers. Table 3.2 shows how the needs and concerns of the baby-boomers have changed as they age.

This population is clearly attracted by different products. The question is – what products are emerging or will emerge to satisfy this group? For example, the 'experience' associated with shopping is an important dimension for this population. Therefore, the more successful stores may want to think about providing a welcoming, 'cocoon' environment, with warm colors and a caring staff. Small gestures that show that you care are important – providing a tea bar rather than a coffee bar, soothing music. This population has time – it does not need to acquire something in a rush and spends for pleasure rather than out of need.

small gestures that show that you care are important

The sport shoe company New Balance is a good example of how successful a company can become if it understands and captures a trend. While New Balance was founded over a century ago, it has only reached

Table 3.2 The changing needs and attitudes of baby boomers

In their youth	Today
Winning	Self-improvement
Self-absorbed	Interested in others
Extreme effort	Balanced effort
Self-serving	Charitable
Physical development	Spiritual development
Disposed to impress others	Authentic
Narcissist	Mature
Extrovert	Introspective
Materialistic	Spiritual
Smell of excitement	Smell of nature
Part of the world	Inner harmony
Indulgence	Care
Ambitous	Realistic
Care for belongings	Detached/care for relationships
Processes	Experiences
Compulsive shoppers	Smart shoppers
Bourgeois	Bohemian
Ambitious	Creative
Productive	Rebellious
Self-discipline	Self-experience
Business	Art
Conservative	Liberal

world-wide success in the past decade. Why? Because it was able to capture a shift in the baby-boomers' frame of mind. The company started a promotion campaign that advertised reasonable training over athletic, extreme performance. The company's advertisements showed people doing sports in their normal, everyday life, rather than super athletes, and their slogan was spot-on: 'Achieve new balance'. Customers felt attracted to this company that seemed to understand their needs, and consequently world sales increased from US$210 million in 1991 to US$1.3 billion in 2003.

In her book, *Clicking*, Faith Popcorn[7] listed some mega-trends in consumer needs/expectations and behaviors that she considered would change the way business is done. Table 3.3 contains a summary of some of these mega-trends.

Now take any four of these trends and apply them to your business. Is your business surfing on them or not? If not, it is high time to start thinking differently!

Table 3.3 Mega-trends in consumer needs/expectations

Trend	Description
Clanning	Driven by need to belong
	Manifestation: boom of writing groups, artist colonies, private clubs, healing clans, internet chats
	Business opportunities: co-housing, mega-bookstores (and other mega-stores that provide the feeling of communal hangout)
Fantasy adventure	Safe thrills and chills to escape stress and boredom
	Manifestation: eating exotic foods, wearing deep dive watches, safe sports, reality TV, obsession with celebrities, with the outdoors
	Business opportunities: selection of exotic foods in supermarkets, original packaging (e.g. wraps), in-line skating, reality shows, discovery channels, makeovers, computer games, stores that let you test the sport gear in 'real world' conditions, boom in amusement parks, 'tough luxe', four-wheel drives
Egonomics	Me, myself and I
	Manifestation: demand for customization, individual attention and personal service
	Business opportunities: shops open later or reorganizing to make shopping easier, all-night diners, on-line newspapers that you can customize to your interests, airlines that remember your preferences, highly specialized widgets (e.g. thinner dental floss for people with tightly spaced teeth)

Table 3.3 *Continued*

Trend	Description
Cashing out	Search for a simpler way of living, opting out of a job, a place, that isn't satisfying Manifestation: growth in entrepreneurship as mistrust of corporations grows, small businesses, moving to the country Business opportunities: magazines around reprioritizing your life, books, consulting. etc. for small business owners, country inns, farms, seed money bank businesses
Vigilant consumer	Consumers acting as pressure groups, using wallets as weapons Manifestation: lack of trust in corporations, substance over style, truth over packaging, chief ethic officers, warrior parents (fighting for children's futures), food cops, etc. Business opportunities: fair trade, non-aggressive toys, environmentally conscious companies
SOS (save our society)	Collective awareness that our environment is constantly degrading Manifestation: consumers attracted to companies that exhibit social conscience: ethics, environment, education, fight to save endangered species, volunteer vacations, charities Business opportunities: emission control on cars, recycling (e.g. Hewlett Packard and cartridges), research in petrol replacement, organic foods, sustainable agriculture

Challenging your business model

This type of visioning input is about reinventing a company business model to outpace competition. For example, after Unilever acquired Best Foods, it ran a visioning process in which the teams were taken to ruins and asked 'What would you do if tomorrow our headquarters were destroyed?' The question was asked to force the teams to rethink their dominant positions and think about what the company would be like if they could start with a clean slate.

In essence, it is about 'easyJetting' your company!

easyJet, or for that matter most low-cost airlines, provided innovation in a fairly mature value market. They did so by taking several bold steps.

a) Targeting a new population: those who travel for pleasure, and who did not fly because it was too expensive. This was a huge untapped market.

b) Offering approximately the same service as the incumbents but at a much cheaper price.

c) Doing even better than the incumbents (dinosaurs) with regard to some benefits, for example safety (new planes) and punctuality (through faster turnaround of the planes on the ground, and planes flying the same route all day, thereby limiting airport delays).

d) Focusing on what is core for short-haul flights: transport from point A to point B. easyJet got rid of all the things that the customer paid extra for (food).

e) Making it simple to buy and use (e-tickets, self-check-in).

f) Eliminating unnecessary cost by either eliminating the service (for example newspapers which, given their size, are difficult to read on a plane, even in business class; or bypassing travel agents), subcontracting it (ground service operated by other companies) or relocating (using cheaper airports where taxes are lower).

Until these airlines redefined what the industry was about and what consumers really cared for, the airline industry seemed set in stone, with constantly spiraling costs and dwindling margins.

The way in which the Japanese beer-making company Asahi challenged incumbent Kirin is another example of how a company can reinvent its position in a mature, highly competitive environment.[8] This example is particularly useful because it is not so much about creating a new product or redesigning the offering within an industry as about capturing what consumers react to. The lessons learnt are applicable to other businesses, independent of industry.

The beer industry in Japan in the late 1980s was an oligopoly, controlled by four main players: Kirin, Sapporo, Suntory and Asahi. At the time, Asahi was positioned well behind the other players – a company that was constantly losing market share and in which different departments spent more time blaming each other for failures than looking outside. They captured 9.6 per cent of the market, while the leader, Kirin, captured 63 per cent. Kirin has been the dominant player in the industry for over 40 years.

In 1986, a new CEO was appointed at the head of Asahi. Hirotaro Higishi immediately set out to change the culture, focusing it on customer needs and trends. He fully supported the development and commercialization of a super dry beer, pulling resources out of different departments and spending virtually all of the company's marketing budget on the new product. The beer was to target the heavy users (males over the age of 40 who drank an average of eight bottles of beer a week, representing 15 per cent of the beer drinking population and 50 per cent of the consumption).

The beer launched on 17 March 1987. Asahi ran advertisements in all five of Japan's major newspapers for over three weeks, and doubled the number of TV advertisements over the same period. The company employed a famous TV journalist, Nobuhiko Ochiai, to promote the beer in the campaign. In retaliation, Kirin launched an advertisement using Gene Hackman. Asahi also distributed over a million free samples all over Japan, collecting consumer feedback.

Demand was so high that Asahi had to stop producing soft juices and turn all of their production plants into breweries. Liquor stores put signs on their doors apologizing for the fact that they were out of Super Dry, and Higishi asked employees not to buy the beer, reserving it for customers. Despite this, they still only managed to respond to 70 per cent of the demand.

While the beer industry grew by 7 per cent that year, Asahi expanded by 34 per cent. While a good beer sold approximately 1 million cases,

Asahi sold 13.5 million cases of the dry beer. By autumn 1988, Asahi had passed the 20 per cent market-share line, and for the first time in 23 years, had beaten Sapporo to become Japan's second largest beer brand. Asahi was by now selling half the dry beer produced in Japan. In 2003, the company overtook Kirin as market leader (40 per cent versus 36 per cent market share).

Asahi's success shows us what happens when a company refuses to accept its given position in an industry and decides to fight back. A number of lessons can be learnt from this case, applicable to other companies in other industries.

❖ Have a superior value proposition that is new and different. Super Dry beer was a brand new concept from the start and recognized as such.

❖ Target the largest existing market segment (in this case, the heavy users).

❖ Use referral/witness/figurehead/opinion leaders to accelerate acceptance. Ochiai was a well-respected and admired figure in Japan.

❖ Balance the marketing mix for consistency and focus – access to the product is key. The packaging of the product and the single message around the beer did this.

❖ Use the general public as your ally to secure free publicity. The public quickly recognized Asahi as the original creator of Super Dry and supported the company by buying its products over the copies from Kirin and Sapporo.

❖ Create some form of scarcity to increase the product fashion effect. Though this was not done intentionally, the way it was handled by Asahi made the product seem precious and desirable.

❖ Free up resources fast somewhere else to focus the efforts and accompany success. Asahi turned all of its production sites into breweries.

These lessons are particularly important for those companies that are squeezed into third place, where they are just large enough to survive but are constantly kept in that position (for example through price wars) by the incumbents.

Internal perceptions

So far, we have looked at inputs from the outside world. We now turn our attention to inside the company and, specifically, to employee perceptions. Perceptions offer valuable information on the gap that often exists between how senior management views the company and how lower level employees view the company.

perceptions offer valuable information on the gap between how senior management views the company and how lower level employees view the company

The flash survey

The flash survey is subjective. It translates what the individuals in your organization think about the company into data that you can use. You may want to ask them what they think is done well or not, where the company is coming from and where it should be headed. As a starting point, you may find it useful to use the flash survey at the end of this chapter. This survey has been used successfully with a wide range of companies.

The flash survey should be distributed first to the people who will participate in the two-day workshop, particularly all those who have a leadership position in the company, and then to as wide an audience as you want. The group of respondents may expand from about 15 to 300 people! Clearly, the more people you involve initially, the easier it will be to share the vision and convince others later. When GrandVision ran the exercise, they sent the survey to the entire executive team, all department heads, store managers and regional managers, a total of 300 people.

The simplicity of the flash survey should not lead you to underestimate its value: with just 13 short answers you are provided with a good idea of your company's perceived strengths and weaknesses and what your employees dream your company can achieve.

Whether you choose to use this survey or another of your own making, a good flash survey should generate answers that are:

- ❖ qualitative
- ❖ short
- ❖ as broad as possible in their scope.

The answers need to be classified before they can be shared during the workshop. This requires grouping them into broad themes, differences and similarities, making sense of what has been said. Try to keep language and differences as close to the original answers as possible. Summarizing dilutes the message. Classifying synonymous words allows you to regroup. For example, if the question is: 'Describe in one word the atmosphere/mood of the company today', you will probably receive a variety of replies that may include the following:

- ❖ energetic
- ❖ dynamic
- ❖ forward-moving
- ❖ fast pace
- ❖ upbeat.

You can then classify around one of the words, choosing the one that is the most representative, without changing what respondents have said. This provides sense without taking away the wealth of perceptions.

Proof reading

Proofs refer to hard data on the actual situation of the company. They are about finding facts that support the perceptions. It requires asking the finance, marketing, R&D and sales departments to present facts. Essentially, each department should answer the question: what have we achieved?

Proofs are also about making sure that the perceptions derived from the flash survey are either corroborated or reinforced by facts. The difference between proofs and perceptions can also teach you a lot about the myths that run through the company – myths that will either help you achieve your vision or are a hurdle to be addressed.

the difference between proofs and perceptions can also teach you a lot about the myths that run through the company

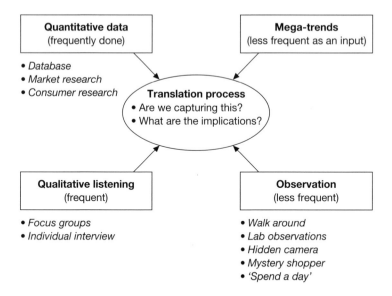

Figure 3.4 Combining different inputs for customer insight

Note: By less frequent we mean methods that are not used a widely and commonly as other tools. For example, most customer-focused companies use some form of market research tool, while fewer look at mega-trends or use mystery shoppers.

For instance, Figure 3.4 shows how these various inputs work together when looking at customers, if customer centricity was at the heart of your business and proofs of it were needed as inputs.

Market and consumer research and focus groups are often used to understand what a company's customers want. However, in the rare cases where the data is acted on, the results rarely provide input on what customers may want *in the future*. Combining the first two methods with an analysis of mega-trends and an observation of how consumers act *in situ* provides four different types of inputs which together give you a clear idea of where your industry is going. They show you where you stand today and where you may stand tomorrow, helping you create a picture of the future.

The dream ticket

We suggest that you begin the workshop with presentations on the topics of proof, perspectives and perceptions to all participants. The order in which you do this is not important. These presentations will take up most of the first day. By the evening, based on the various inputs, the team should be able to draft a dream with a deadline.

The second day focuses on agreeing on the vision, deciding on key ways, milestones and actions, and determining desired behaviors. At the end of the second day, the team agrees on the next steps – i.e. how the vision will be communicated to the rest of the organization. Figure 3.5 shows a suggested agenda for running the two-day workshop.

Step 1: Sharing the data

sharing the achievements of the company will help build a common awareness that is often lacking

Proofs. Starting the day with proofs is a good way of grounding the reality. It is particularly important to share the achievements of the company. This will help build a common awareness that is often lacking, because each

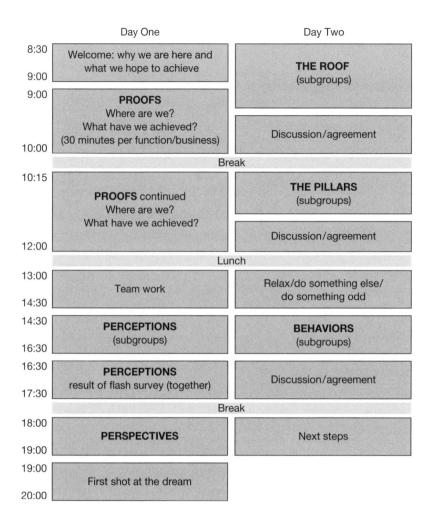

Figure 3.5 Suggested schedule for a two-day workshop

individual focuses primarily on his business or function. Typically, the executive committee will know of new product launches and key financial indicators, but will be aware of very little else beyond that. The different functions must understand how the organization as a whole has succeeded or failed, beyond financial measures or marketing metrics. This helps to break the pigeon-holes in the company.

Perceptions. The perceptions gathered from across the organization need to be shared with the team – the 'almost new' data helps mirror where the company stands at that specific point in time.

As we noted above, try not to summarize the different perceptions too much, for you may be accused of making generalizations from the specific. Also, the diversity of the responses may be very informative. When this exercise was run with Euro Disney, using the 12-point questionnaire, and with 84 participants, the answers to the flash survey generated 25 visions, 165 strategies and 26 desired behaviors! It required a lot of energy and focus to come up with a single dream, three key ways and five behaviors!

If the team is a large one, allow for subgroup work to analyze the perceptions before going into the plenary session. Often, the results come as a surprise, and the subgroups allow participants to share emotions before regrouping. The surprise factor is usually a result of:

❖ breadth of answers but no contradictions among them
❖ contradictory answers
❖ negative answers.

The first indicates a lack of focus and slack in the tightness of execution. It is the easiest to solve by refocusing everyone. The second means that there are some conflicting views about where the company is, or should be, going. Hopefully, the data and the perspectives will get people to share more of a common viewpoint. The third is almost certainly an indication that part of the senior team will need to/want to leave.

Perspectives. Here you want to share a common picture of the future, generating discussions based on the types of inputs we suggested. It may be interesting to provide both conventional and unconventional approaches to what the future may hold by inviting outside speakers.

The work on proofs, perceptions and perspectives, which leads to taking a first shot at the dream, will take you to the end of the first day.

The evening should be dedicated to the roof (creating a dream with a deadline). This will allow people to think it over during the night. The risk is that giving the team time to think about the roof makes it harder to reach an agreement – each individual being inspired differently by the inputs of the day. But the team must be given the time to reflect on what it has learnt during the day and the implications of that on the future of the company.

the team must be given the time to reflect on what it has learnt during the day

Having said that, if the team can agree on the dream, it is easier to converge on the other elements of the house (key ways, milestones, behaviors). One of the best ways of getting agreement is to divide the team into subgroups (3–5 groups) that discuss in small teams and then confer on the basics of the dream. We recommend that the CEO be present throughout the first day. Essentially, he or she will serve as referee, and will make the final call when the groups come back with recommendations for the dream.

Step 2: Raising the roof

The morning of the second day focuses on the pillars and the desired behaviors – those that will support the execution of the vision. The afternoon should be dedicated to agreeing on how to enlist the organization and communicate the vision.

We suggest you devote the morning to the pillars, milestones and behaviors. The pillars can be created using small teams, with the CEO serving as referee. Do not work by functions – you need an approach that is corporate or business-unit wide. Ask the teams to work on the key ways (the headings of each of the three pillars) before working on the milestones and actions. Remind them that the columns must be balanced in terms of number of action points and level of detail.

The main challenge will be to synthesize the different approaches – to distill the divergent viewpoints into a coherent whole. It is clear that you should not impose what the three pillars should be about. They have to fit logically with the dream. The language used must be straight-forward – everyone in the company should be **what is important is the convergence between the three key ways** able to understand it and remember the dream and the three key ways. What is impor-tant is the convergence between the three key ways: do these three columns lead to a corpo-rate or competitive advantage? Is there unity? Are they the best way for us to reach our destination?

Throughout the morning you need to ask yourself these questions:

- ❖ Do these key ways support my vision?
- ❖ Are they essential to success in our business?
- ❖ Have we missed anything more important?

You must then apply the same discipline to the milestones and actions in each of the pillars.

- ❖ Are they sufficiently measurable that if we revisit our vision in six months, or one year, or two years, and we look at our achievements, we will be able to determine whether we have reached our objectives or not?
- ❖ Do we have them all?
- ❖ Are there things that we are refraining from doing immediately?
- ❖ Is there a sequence of implementation?
- ❖ Are there things that we can leave until next year?

The problem is often to look beyond the first year – it requires vision and risk-taking.

The afternoon should be devoted to behaviors and winning over the organization. Ask yourself and the team the same type of questions as you agree on supporting behaviours. We would recommend that you settle for a maximum of five behaviors. A laundry list of 'desired behavior' blurs focus and makes progress harder to measure.

Sharing the vision will be covered in Chapter 4, which is dedicated exclusively to this topic. The chapter covers the language used to describe the vision; how and by whom the vision should be cascaded down into the organization; how to obtain commitment and what the implications for action are. Never forget – 'action goes where the money flows'. When sharing the vision across the organization, it **'action goes where the money flows'** is important not to lose momentum, and bank on the enthusiasm generated by the workshop.

Quality versus quantity

The participants are the leaders who will inspire their teams. It is therefore clear that the process is heavily influenced by the quality of the leaders who are in charge of developing the dream, sharing it and implementing it.

Choosing whom to invite to the workshop is a balancing act: the greater the number of participants, the easier it is to get commitment, but there is a limit to the number of people who can contribute to a one-page vision. We believe that a good sized group includes the CEO, the executive committee (functions) and the heads of regions. In total this may represent a team of approximately 40 to 80 people. What is important is to get input **get input from field** from field representatives – the last thing you **representatives** want is an ivory tower vision!

CEO as householder

During the course of the workshop, the CEO plays the role of referee, and has the final say. However, the CEO also plays an important role as the 'owner' of the workshop. As such, this person should:

❖ Explain to the audience why the workshop is happening.

❖ Emphasize his/her personal commitment to making it happen.

❖ Emphasize that the visioning process is happening 'here and now' and that there will be no second chances to discuss and disagree.

❖ Introduce the facilitators, if any, and the guest speakers.

❖ Thank the team for participating.

The participation of the CEO clearly demonstrates commitment to the process. At the end of the two-day workshop, the CEO should ask the participants whether they are comfortable with the new vision or not, and whether they are ready to execute it. This is why it is critical that the CEO owns the entire process. Only he or she can demand this level of commitment from the senior team, and provide credibility to the exercise.

Summary

This chapter describes the visioning process that leads to the design of the vision. We argue that a vision does not need to take months to complete. In fact, we think a vision can be designed over the course of two days. Obviously, some initial preparation needs to be done: collecting information on the actual state of the company; inviting those who will participate in the two-day workshop; and gathering information for the different types of inputs that will stimulate thinking. The size of the group participating can vary, but should at least include all of the senior executive committee, the CEO, regional heads and preferably the board members.

The first of the two days should be spent on looking at three types of input that provide everyone with a very complete picture of the company, its environment and where it might be going in the future. We group these inputs into three categories:

❖ **Proofs** are about hard facts: the financial position of the company, its achievements and shortcomings.

❖ **Perceptions** focus on how your employees view your company, using the results of a flash survey.

❖ **Perspectives** provide 'out of the box' thinking on the company and its industry. This can include mega-trends, scenarios or easyJetting your business.

The first day ends with a draft of your 'dream with a deadline'. This gives participants the night to reflect on the previous day, and allows time for everyone to raise questions. Obtaining commitment at this point is very important, as it will facilitate agreeing on key ways and supporting behaviors.

The second day starts with getting commitment to a common vision and then moving on to agree on key ways, milestones and actions, and defining desired behaviors. Finally, the team should discuss how it will share the vision with the rest of the organization.

During the course of the workshop, the CEO plays the role of referee, making the final call.

Example of the flash survey

On the [date], your company management will meet to discuss your 'vision for the future', i.e. how you intend to take the company forward.

I will be facilitating the discussion. Your inputs are very important as visions are easier to implement if they are shared; and it starts with getting inputs from all managers.

It should not take you more than ten minutes to answer all the questions. Please return the survey directly to me by e-mail: [name of facilitator]

Thank you very much in advance.
[signature]

Example of the flash survey *(continued)*

A VISION FOR THE FUTURE FOR *X*
FLASH SURVEY

1. Describe in three words where your company was three years ago.
    _____
    _____
    _____

2. Identify three major accomplishments the company has achieved during the last three years.
    _____
    _____
    _____

3. Determine the three major current strengths of your company.
    _____
    _____
    _____

4. Identify three major shortcomings (weaknesses).
    _____
    _____
    _____

5. Characterize in two words the working climate at your company.
    _____
    _____
    _____

6. Characterize in two words the management style at your company.
    _____
    _____
    _____

7. What values (beliefs) are currently promoted at your company?
    _____
    _____
    _____

▶

Example of the flash survey *(continued)*

8. What is your biggest concern today?

   _____
   _____
   _____

9. What excites you most?

   _____
   _____
   _____

10. Describe where the company should be tomorrow (i.e. in three years) using inspiring words (what is your dream with a deadline for the company?).

    _____
    _____
    _____

11. List three key ways which should be used by the company to achieve this dream.

    _____
    _____
    _____

12. Identify five behaviors that must be around to promote the success of this dream.

    _____
    _____
    _____

13. What new values should be particularly developed at the company ?

    _____
    _____
    _____

    Are you: ☐ Head office   ☐ Field   ☐ Unit manager

    Thank you for replying before [date] so that we have time for analysis before the seminar planned on [date]. Please send by e-mail to [name of facilitator].

NOTES TO CHAPTER 3

1   William Hutchinson Murray (1951). *The Scottish Himalayan Expedition*. J. M. Dent & Sons Ltd.

2   Paul Strebel (2006). Scenario planning. IMD exercises. Powerpoint presentation.

3   Jo Johnson (2005). Directors target India for board meetings. *Financial Times*, 21 November.

4   Company documents.

5   Family owned, 18,000 employees, sales €2.2 billion in 2004.

6   Baby boomers are given different names in different countries: silver generation in Japan, golden oldies in the US, papy-boomers in France.

7   Faith Popcorn and Lys Marigold (1998). *Clicking: 17 Trends That Drive Your Business*. Collins.

8   Dominique Turpin, Kirin Brewery Co. Limited. The dry beer war. IMD 5–0394, 2002.

4 Sharing the dream

*I believe that this nation should commit itself to achieving
the goal, before this decade is out, of landing a man on
the moon and returning him safely to the earth.*

PRESIDENT JOHN F. KENNEDY, MESSAGE TO CONGRESS, 25 MAY 1961

Kennedy's famous speech about putting a man on the moon is a masterful example of a leader sharing a dream. Notice how it is directed not to any one group of Americans but to the nation as a whole. What all great visions have in common is the ability to unite diverse groups in a common cause. It is this unity behind a grand design that makes a vision

all great visions have in common the ability to unite diverse groups in a common cause

such a powerful leadership tool. The same principle applies in business. If a vision is to become a leadership tool, then everyone in the business has to share in it.

In the first three chapters, we have looked at what makes a good vision, how to work with the House Model and the two-day process that leads to defining the vision. The next four chapters will look at how you implement the vision, first through sharing the vision, and then through organizational design, discipline and continuous transformation.

In this chapter we look at sharing the vision across the organization. This involves the language used, the tools for communicating the vision and how to get everyone on board, including how to present the vision to the board and gaining their commitment to your dream. Understanding why a company has chosen a specific path generates a feeling of ownership and allows everyone to take initiatives, experiment and propose new ways. We then look at the tools that help cascade the vision across the organization and the importance of internalizing the vision. Finally, we discuss how to deal with those who do not share your vision and how to keep the dream alive.

Day-dream believers

If you cannot persuade everyone in the company to dream with you, enthuse about the dream and commit to a common future, the vision will not happen. It is sharing the vision that makes it successful. Sharing the vision is about:

- ❖ understanding it
- ❖ approving it (but with commitment, not compliance)
- ❖ agreeing on the implications for action.

Understanding is primarily about language. So your first step after the two-day workshop is to deal with the language of the vision. We recommend that you nominate a small team of three people who will work on refining the wording of the vision, as it was drafted during the workshop. Its terminology must be simple and clear enough for everyone in the organization to understand and remember it. The final version must be communicated back to the original team, including the new wording and any inputs from the board. We recommend that you run an 'idiot test' – show the vision to a group of people who have not seen it before and ask them:

- ❖ Is the language simple and clear enough?
- ❖ Do you understand it?
- ❖ Do you find the vision exciting, inspiring and meaningful?
- ❖ Is it to the point?
- ❖ Does it provide sufficient guidance as to what the priorities are?
- ❖ Does it provide sufficient guidance as to what initiatives they can embrace to contribute?

Once approved, the vision can be cascaded across the organization. The cascading process is the linchpin of the entire sharing process. The team involved in the visioning process needs to agree on *how, by whom* and *how far* the vision will be cascaded through the organization.

❖ Who will share with whom?

❖ What process will be used to get feedback?

❖ What format, or formats will be used to disseminate the vision (a text, a drawing, a movie?) and where?

Obviously, the format depends on the target. We look at this in greater detail later in this chapter.

What is equally important is to carefully think through when and by whom the vision will be shared. This must be planned thoroughly, for maximum impact, consistency and focus. The vision should NOT be communicated by your communications department or through an outside agency. The top team who defined it (i.e. participants in the visioning process workshop) must demonstrate that they own the vision, that they believe in it and that they are going to make it happen.

the vision should NOT be communicated by your communications department or through an outside agency

Having the top team share the vision is the best way of obtaining commitment. You must be able to defend it, answering questions around why you chose this vision and not another one. The last thing you want is compliance. Everyone needs to believe in the vision. They must feel committed, and they must want to make that dream with a deadline become a reality. In Chapter 6, we will look at some of the actions and behaviors that can kill a vision. We will see that many of these have to do with lack of understanding and lack of commitment to the vision.

everyone needs to believe in the vision

Finally, you need to address the implications for action:

❖ Does your new vision change the way you do business?

❖ What concrete actions/initiatives need to be taken?

❖ What initiatives to you expect people to come up with within the set framework?

❖ What empowerment is acceptable?

❖ What actions are included from the vision?

❖ How are you going to measure progress?

❖ Under what circumstances will you decide to change the vision?

❖ What will the implications be for the next letter of intent? Budget? Personal objectives?

You should consider the implications for actions before the end of the workshop. One approach is for each participant to agree on a list of actions that they will commit to for themselves and their team. Each team will then use the same approach back in their business unit – cascading the action lists down across the organization. Each one of these actions must be included in the normal budgeting process. For example, if getting closer to your customers means designing a new website, the budget for its development must be approved at all the right levels in the organization. Problems with the implementation of a vision begin with small things like someone refusing to sign off the development of a customer-friendly website.

The entire process – from the moment the vision is crafted to the time when it is cascaded across the organization – should not exceed two months. Any longer than this, and the momentum and interest in the visioning process are lost.

Back it or sack it

Ideally the board, or some representative, should be present during the entire visioning process. However, their participation can be problematic for several reasons. First, some boards are very short-term oriented, and are not interested in this type of exercise in the future. Second, it can be difficult for a board to commit to two full days. Third, in some cases the board's preferred 'management' style is that of referee, rather

than proactive intervention in strategic thinking. So building a dream using a leadership
tool that leads to commitment and excitement
will seem utopian to some members as a part
of the normal duties of management. Dreams
tend to take second place behind EBITs and
ROIs. To some extent, how and how much

**building a dream
using a leadership tool
that leads to
commitment and
excitement will seem
utopian to some
members**

you share of the vision will depend on how you use your board – some
CEOs work with their boards on a regular basis on long-term thinking,
others only share quarterly results, risks and investment approvals.

So how do you win your board over to your vision, when they have not
had the advantage of going through a two-day visioning process?

First, you need to convince them of the validity and soundness of
your vision. How do you do this? There are several ways in which you
can present the vision, depending on the style of your board and your
relationship with its members. You may want to start with a short introduction on why the company needs a vision. The main arguments
should include the need for alignment and for focusing energies on a
clear and exciting goal. You could also skip this introduction and go
straight to the vision and the key ways, involving your board by asking
them direct questions:

❖ What do you think?

❖ Does it tell a clear story of our next steps in the coming 3–5 years?

❖ Does it convey a good idea of where you want to go and where
you don't want to go?

❖ Are the key ways representative of the key components of your
competitive advantage for each business (and corporate
advantage for a multibusiness)?

❖ Have you forgotten any key milestones, actions?

❖ Can it excite financial analysts as well?

❖ What would you add/remove?

❖ Do you approve?

❖ What are you going to do with it?

Alternatively, especially if your board is far removed from an in-depth knowledge of your operation, you could choose to use a deductive approach, by which you summarize the thinking process you and your team went through to formulate your vision:

❖ Current situation.

❖ Why the situation is not satisfactory.

❖ Let us project our ambitions into the future.

❖ What will the vision lead us to do differently.

In this case, you may want to share the full picture, using a summary of the different inputs that were presented at the seminar, how you reached agreement on the vision, key ways and behaviors. This deductive approach is particularly good if your board is essentially a 'financial controller' board, i.e. if in one way or another, your company is a subsidiary to a financial holding or to private equity investors.

At the end of the discussion ask your board for their reactions, and for approval. Together, you agree on the next steps and how to integrate the vision with the budget. It is important to recognize that, while you have spent two days on the process, you will **you will probably have less than an hour or two to convince your board of the soundness of your dream** probably have less than an hour or two to convince your board of the soundness of your dream. Furthermore, the board will not be familiar with this type of approach, but more with the classical approach, which is incremental – buy this company, sell that division, as would exist in the SWOT analysis. It is easier for the board to approve a plan that says 'Last year we acquired three companies, this year we should acquire another four' than a vision that says 'I will be No. 1 in Europe in five years from now'.

Part of the issue is linked to how comfortable you feel with your board: for example, if you are unsure as to how they might respond, you may want to approach each member individually, testing the water, or you may choose to approach those who are most likely to influence the rest of the group. This will help you assess the type of reaction to expect when you present to the board.

There is, of course, the very real risk that the board will reject the vision, in which case you have three options:

❖ Drop your vision.

❖ Revise your vision.

❖ Resign.

It is your responsibility as an executive team to assess each board member and how they might respond to your vision. Therefore, if they reject it, you should probably consider resigning. It is a clear indication that you are not supported by your board. However, most of the time the board trusts the CEO and he or she delivers results (otherwise the person would get fired anyway). But you do want to avoid reaching the situation where the board quashes something you have spent two days creating, for lack of common ground – because if that does happen, you will probably lose most of your senior management team, who were excited and now feel betrayed.

One solution, if you believe that the board may reject your vision but you and your team feel strongly about its validity, is to share only what you must. You could share only the short-term results and action plans. If you know for sure that the series of incremental steps you have or will define with your team (the letters of intent) will lead to your dream, you may not necessarily have to share the dream itself – because if you do not achieve your short-term results they will come back to you with your dream and demand an explanation. In most cases, however, it is hard to argue against the fact that a committed, energized organization is more likely to achieve the desired objective.

a committed, energized organization is more likely to achieve the desired objective

This is not about hiding your vision from the board but instead about sharing only the steps that lead to it. Because if you do try to hide your vision completely from the board you can be sure that someone will stab you in the back. The case of Philippe Bourguignon, ex-CEO of Club Med, serves as a warning to all. While Bourguignon was away on a business trip, his subordinate, Henri Giscard d'Estaing, (whom he had personally appointed against the will of some of the board members), went to the club's key shareholder and board member, and said 'I disagree with his vision – choose between us'. Upon returning from his trip, Bourguignon met with the chairman of the board and the key shareholder. Informed of the situation, he refused to defend himself and left the company.[1]

In some cases, management suffers from the dilemma of not delivering on short-term results, while still having to think ahead, showing the team that there is light at the end of the tunnel. This light is what helps people keep a high level of energy at times when decisions are short-term, around cost-cutting, dismissals, downsizing, etc.

In these situations, going to the board with a vision will either make them laugh if they have a sense of humor or otherwise seriously doubt the mental ability of their senior management team.

In such situations we recommend that you add a fourth pillar to the House Model. This fourth pillar actually looks more like a front-piece. It will essentially be expressed as a precondition for the rest to happen, as shown in Figure 4.1.

This formula is more acceptable internally because it clearly states the need to take short-term, painful actions to produce results before going forward. It also generates the 'hope' of more exciting things to come if this precondition is fulfilled. It is also more acceptable for the board, because it places the vision in perspective.

Whatever approach you choose, stand firm:

- ❖ Be concrete.
- ❖ Use images to describe where you want to be.
- ❖ Present the vision as a pitch to your own people: be convincing.
- ❖ Sell it: show your energy and your enthusiasm.
- ❖ Remind the board of the process followed before and after approval.
- ❖ Ask them not to play 'word-games' with the vision – it is not meant to exist in an advertising context. It is meant to exist as an inspiring and concrete message that takes the company forward with both focus and excitement.

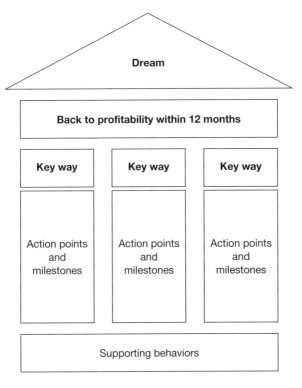

Figure 4.1 A dream with a precondition

Do not forget that while the board elects the CEO, the CEO also appoints the board members.

Selling the dream

Having obtained the go-ahead from the board and from the team that designed the vision, you can now cascade the vision across the organization. This is done by those who participated in the workshop along with their teams. In some cases, you may also want to adapt the vision to the audience, essentially in terms of vocabulary, although obviously it is better to retain the same language throughout. Other points you should consider as you roll out the vision are:

- ❖ Include it immediately in any induction program for new employees that you may have.

- ❖ Use it as a stretch goal, a challenge, which the entire organization will be rewarded for achieving (and therefore linking it to the incentive/bonus system).

Some people argue that because the vision represents the company's strategy it should be kept secret, but we believe that it should be seen everywhere within the organization – on the walls of the cafeteria, in the factories and offices. You cannot implement a vision by just looking at words.

you cannot implement a vision by just looking at words

There are no set rules for cascading, except that the more people understand where a company is heading, the easier it will be for them to find ways of making it happen. The limit to how far down you cascade is the point at which, if you go further, the answer to the basic question of 'How does this do something for my competitive advantage (at the business unit level) or corporate advantage (at the corporate level)?' is a clear 'nothing'.

Cascading starts with each member of the original design team. Each member of that team is responsible for presenting the vision to his own team, and they to their teams and so on (see Figure 4.2).

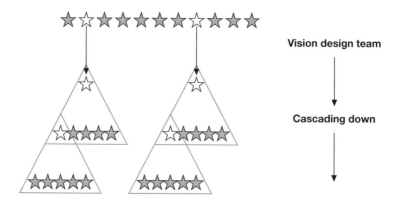

Figure 4.2 Cascading the vision

The cascading exercise should not simply be a presentation: it must be an opportunity for discussion, allowing both parties to identify three areas for action:

- ❖ Actions that need to be taken by the business unit, and which will be used as inputs in the next letter of intent/budgeting process. This is the reason why it is best to plan the visioning process so that it precedes the normal annual process.

- ❖ Originate initiatives that are needed to support the vision: normally, they are already identified in the three pillars but can be further specified in terms of who will take charge of what, and when. Other elements can also be discussed during the cascading process, including new incentive systems, new HR processes, new policies and procedures.

- ❖ Behavioral changes. Each member of the team and every team should identify what it can do more of (or sometimes less of!), in terms of behaviors in order to support and align with the new behaviors required by the vision.

To give you an idea of time-frame and size, a company of 10,000 employees may run anything from 5 to 1,000 forums in a 1–3-month time-frame.

The cascade approach is used to communicate the 'why', i.e. the direction the company is going in for the next 3–5 years. This sets the context within which all actors will align and competitive advantage will be reinforced; and this is at the heart of your organization. You should not use outside consultants to communicate this 'why' because it would mean delegating the single most important thing to outside leadership. For example, Jack Welch spent 30 per cent of his time at GE's corporate university, Crotonville, sharing his vision for the company. By doing this as a CEO:

- ❖ you transfer know-how, attitudes and perspectives;
- ❖ if you have to spend time convincing others, you end up convincing yourself.

some communication tools can help the vision become an integral part of the fabric of the organization

Some communication tools can help the vision become an integral part of the fabric of the organization. In 1993, when Euro Disney embarked on its vision 'Let's win the hearts of Europe by 1996', it had to convince its 12,000 cast members to play the game and win, and do so by 1996. As a first step it restructured its massive organization into 250 smaller units, with 250 managers in charge of implementing the vision. They were called the 'Small World Managers'. These small world managers participated in a 20-day executive program that was split into three parts – each part focusing on one of the three pillars of the vision. Every executive vice-president and vice-president cascaded the vision to the level of those 250 managers, who in turn presented it to the 50 cast members who reported to them. The vision also became part of all the training programs of the Disney University, including the two-day induction program for new cast members.

The message was further reinforced via posters everywhere 'backstage'. Among other things, a giant house (four meters by six meters) was built and placed at the entrance of the main cafeteria, where 6,000 meals were served every day. A smaller version was also placed in front of other, smaller, cafeterias. In this particular case, Disney used four tools: cascading by the senior team, visual props, communication through the Disney University and the in-depth training of the 250 small world managers. By 1995, the company was two years ahead of its objective in terms of both financial and customer satisfaction results. There are other examples:

> In the factory of a construction materials company in Holland, a giant representation of the vision was put up inside the plant, so that all the employees could visualize it and discuss it.

> A financial services company decided to design a 'gold' chocolate bar, on which the vision was inscribed. Every single one of the company's 70,000 employees received the bar.

Without having to be gimmicky, support through impactful communication is an essential part of the cascading process. It is crucial to ensuring that everyone knows the vision, is excited and inspired by it, and wants to contribute.

Gotta luv it

To a large extent, the success of your vision will depend on how well your employees internalize its message and the corresponding desired behaviors, and are sufficiently inspired and excited by it that it guides their actions and behaviors, both internally and externally. When employees understand, and 'live' a vision, their behaviors and attitudes help crystallize a clear image of what the company stands for in the minds of customers and employees alike.

All internal communication must reinforce the vision and the desired behaviors, consistently and frequently. This means that the messages need to be designed proactively, from the top down, in the cascading manner that we described above.

In an article published in 1995 about the culture at SouthWest Airlines, Sandra Miles and Glynn Maygold[2] suggested that consistency and frequency of messages helped create a strong bond between the organization and its employees, what they called a positive psychological contract. Respect of the contract generates trust, influences productivity positively, and affects how employees work together and with their customers. Inconsistent messages, however, generate confusion and a sense of distrust, negatively influencing turnover, productivity and loyalty.

inconsistent messages generate confusion and a sense of distrust

SouthWest Airlines is a good example of a company whose employees live the company's vision and values. The airline has been among the top performing stocks over the past 30 years and has made a profit every year since 1973. The company was cited in the 100 Best Corporate Citizens from 2000 to 2005,[3] and was also given the Performance through People Award in 2004.[4] The award honours companies that successfully capitalize on the human interactions that affect a company's long-term growth. SouthWest was also recognized as the most admired airline in the world from 1997 to 2003. The company had the lowest employee turnover and the highest employee satisfaction rate in the industry (turnover of 5 per cent compared to an industry average of 20–30 per cent). In parallel, the airline received less than one complaint for every 10,000 passengers boarded. The philosophy of the company was reflected in its mission statement, including both customers and the company employees.

The mission of SouthWest Airlines is dedication to the highest quality of customer service delivered with a sense of warmth, friendliness, individual pride and 'company spirit'.

To Our Employees

We are committed to provide our Employees a stable work environment with equal opportunity for learning and personal growth. Creativity and innovation are encouraged for improving the effectiveness of SouthWest Airlines. Above all, Employees will be provided the same concern, respect, and caring attitude within the organization that they are expected to share externally with every SouthWest Customer.

Source: southwest.com/about_swa/mission.html.

SouthWest clearly puts its employees first, above and beyond its clients, with the expectation that employees will in return treat their clients as well as they themselves are treated. Customer service and customer orientation are explicit in everything the company does.[5] Employees are motivated to deliver high levels of service, and know that their efforts will be recognized and rewarded. The high levels of motivation lead to operational efficiency and to the friendly service upheld in the mission statement.

The company's values include fun, love (which they call LUV, being Texan), team spirit and altruism, with supporting values that help deliver the mission statement: profitability, cost-effective operations, family, hard work, individuality, ownership, egalitarianism, common sense and simplicity. The values are communicated using simple statements such as 'Positively outrageous service' or 'SouthWest Spirit', so that employees know exactly what is expected of them, both internally and externally.

Messages are consistent both internally and externally, from the human resource (HR) policies that support the company's values to the advertising campaigns and the stock exchange ticker, both under the theme of LUV. For example, in 2000, the company ran parallel internal and external campaigns on the theme of freedom: externally to reflect that low fares allow people to travel to places they would not be able to travel to otherwise, and internally to communicate the freedom to grow and develop as an individual.

Future employees are carefully assessed to ensure that their personal values are completely in synch with the organizational values. Employees who have been with the company for nine months or less are invited to have lunch with the executive team, to discuss how well their expectations have been met and how well they fit into the corporate culture.

Compensation is also used to reinforce the message. In addition to stock options and profit-sharing, some compensation schemes clearly support the organizational values: for example, pilots are paid by the flight rather than by the hour. As a result, they proactively look for cost-saving solutions, from flying at lower altitudes to asking for a runway closer to the hangar.

Best practice is shared across the organization in a monthly publication, along with stories of employees who provided positively outrageous customer service. Team leaders are carefully selected as they are seen as ambassadors for the company's culture. Supervisors are encouraged to constantly reinforce the corporate values and employees are encouraged to go above their personal boss if they feel that the vision and values are not respected.

Customer letters, both negative and positive, are widely shared. Employees involved in bad service cases are asked for their insight as to how this happened and could be avoided in the future. They are not fired or stigmatized.

The SouthWest case demonstrates concretely some of the points we have been making: the importance of focus, commitment (not compliance) energy and enthusiasm, as well as setting new boundaries for your business. Who would have thought, 20 years ago, that low-cost airlines would succeed and make more money than the regular airlines! Only visionary thinking could come to that conclusion!

Great expectations

> We never set out to build a brand. Our goal was to build a great
> company, one that stood for something, one that valued the
> authenticity of its products and the passion of its people.
>
> HOWARD SCHULTZ[6]

When everyone in a company is focused on a single goal, the energy and enthusiasm generated spills over to create enthusiasm with consumers. Starbucks, for example, built a brand starting with its employees, not its customers. Howard Schultz, CEO of Starbucks, believed that the best way to exceed customer expectations was to hire and train very good people, have them embrace the passion for coffee and not try to sell yet another cup of coffee. He built the company around a values-centered culture, at the base of which were respect and dignity for all employees at all levels.

Starting from these values, he built coffee houses that were about an 'experience', a haven between home and office where you could have an excellent cup of coffee in a friendly atmosphere. For example, because coffee was the first thing that you should hit you when you walk into a Starbucks, employees were asked not to wear perfume, the shops were entirely non-smoking areas and no soup or cooked foods were on sale.

Behind every decision was a clear vision. While the company counted on word-of-mouth from satisfied customers, it also hired local public relations (PR) agencies to understand local concerns and heritage, and the first shop in any location was always on a high street. Openings were turned into media affairs, inviting friends and partners of employees who lived in the city, shareholders, mail order customers and members of the causes they sponsored.

The Starbucks example shows how enthusiasm and commitment to a dream (the best cup of coffee in the best location) lead to success. It also demonstrates the importance of supporting values and behaviors.

Insomniacs need not apply

Those who do not share the dream should be let go. No question about it. You will not get focus, alignment and good execution if executives and employees at all levels continue to go in different directions. It is your challenge to involve people in defining the vision, to explain it and try to convince everyone about where the dream is taking the company, but you cannot compromise on commitment – everyone has to want to go in the same direction – 'Let's make half of the dream come true' is NOT an option.

'let's make half the dream come true' is NOT an option

In most cases, those who do not believe in the new vision will choose to leave of their own accord, particularly those who were involved in the visioning process described in Chapter 3.

There are some clear signs that your vision has not been bought into:

❖ Bad-mouthing right after the two-day workshop.
❖ No shift in the allocation of resources during the next letter of intent/budgeting process.
❖ No observable change in behavior.

Let us return to our Euro Disney example and their vision of 'Let's win the hearts of Europe'. This is clearly an emotional rather than a rational statement – it focused on customers more than finance, on a winning spirit rather than purely managerial support. One of the most important tools for 'winning' was to turn the park into an all-season resort, encouraging people to come to Euro Disney throughout the year. This could not happen unless the creative team in charge of launching new parades, shows, etc., and the marketing team in charge of packaging, communication and pricing worked together to spread the events across the four seasons. This called for very close relationships and integration ('us') between the creative team and the marketing people, collaborating to link events to one another. To make sure that the collaboration happened, those who did not think in terms of 'us' (let *us* win ...) were fired. At the end of the first year of implementation, 35 out of 84 senior executives had left. At the same time, the company had increased sales and customers by 10 per cent and for the first time since opening, and ahead of the recovery plan, profits were achieved.

It is sometimes difficult to know whether you have buy-in and commitment before it is too late. How will you know that the vision is in everybody's mind and that everyone agrees with it? You need to check constantly that everyone knows the vision and defends it. Never stop asking: in the elevator, in the cafeteria, at the end of induction programs, on the shop floor. Always ask 'What is our dream for our company? What are the three things we need to do to get there? What behaviors will support it?' Alignment requires focus, and focus requires single-mindedness. Everyone must be single-mindedly focused on making the vision happen.

everyone must be single-mindedly focused on making the vision happen

Keeping the dream alive

The vision has been approved by the board, cascaded across the organization, and included in all aspects of how the company does business. The risk is to start taking it for granted, without checking the reality. It is critical that the vision is reviewed on a yearly basis, by those who designed it, and its progress assessed:

- ❖ What have we achieved? Accomplished?
- ❖ Are we off? If yes, why?
- ❖ Are we late? If yes, why?
- ❖ What should we do/what do we need to do to get back on track?
- ❖ How do we translate the necessary actions in the letter of intent?

❖ Do we need to add actions without changing the dream? (best option – tenacity pays)

❖ Do we need to give up on the dream? (last resort – stubbornness does not pay)

The critical question is always whether you are on track or not. The updates serve as indicators of what may still be needed to make the dream happen. If you have reached the date stated in your vision without completing your dream, DO NOT DROP IT – add a year. You will lose all credibility with your team if you drop your dream so close to the goal.

In a retail company, the dream stated that, within five years, 1,000 people would be generating €100 million in sales. The CEO announced to everyone that if the objective was reached, all 1,000 employees would be invited to Agadir, Morocco, to celebrate. The fifth year was 2003. The company reached €93 million. The CEO did not drop the vision, he added another year, giving everyone the opportunity to ride camels on the beaches of Agadir!

However, it may be that your vision changes because you have made a large acquisition or there are important disruptions in your market. An acquisition always comes as a surprise, because you rarely know beforehand (3–5 years before, when you created the vision) what might be for sale. If the acquisition or disruption is significant, it will change the scope of your business, and a new dream will be necessary.

Summary

There are three key aspects to sharing the vision across the organization. This first of these is about the language, ensuring that the vision is clear and simple, while generating enthusiasm and energy. The second is about by whom, to whom and how the vision is communicated. The format chosen should be visually arresting. The vision should be shared with the organization via the top team though a cascading process with some communications support. Finally, sharing the vision is also about

sharing the vision is about understanding the implications for actions

understanding the implications for actions: how does the new vision change the way we do business and behave?

If the board did not participate in the visioning process leading to the dream, it is important that you get their buy-in. How much and how you share the vision with the board will depend on your relationship with the board – you could share the entire process that led to the design of the vision, including the different types of inputs; you could choose to explain the need for a new vision or you could dive straight into the vision, key ways and behaviors. If the board rejects your vision, you should probably consider resigning.

Assuming that you have obtained approval from the board, you can cascade the vision across the organization. Cascading the vision is about explaining the 'why'. Ideally, the senior team cascades down to their team, which cascades down to theirs, and so on. The cascading exercise is an opportunity for discussion. In the course of the process, team leaders and their team members should agree on:

- ❖ the responsibility for the initiatives defined in the pillars that will help support the vision;
- ❖ the actions that need to be taken by the business units as support for the initiatives, and which will be used as inputs in the budgeting process;
- ❖ how to align behaviors with the vision.

Communication tools help translate and cascade the vision across the organization. Beyond communication through senior management, these include visual props and gimmicks and induction programs.

It is important that all your employees internalize the vision. When everyone lives and breathes the vision, they generate an enthusiasm which is shared by the company's clients. This is why those who do not share the vision should be fired.

Finally, it is important to measure progress regularly, looking at the achievements versus the strategy and making changes where necessary.

NOTES TO CHAPTER 4

1   Philippe Bourguignon (2005) *Hop!* Anne Carrière.

2   Sandra Jeanquart Miles and W. Glynn Mangold (2005). Positioning SouthWest Airlines through employee branding. *Business Horizons*, 48, 535–45;
    Kevin Freiberg and Jackie Freiberg (1998). *Nuts! SouthWest Airlines' Crazy Recipe for Business and Personal Success.* Broadway.
    Jody Hoffer Gittel (2002). *The SouthWest Airlines Way: Using the Power of Relationships to Achieve High Performance.* McGraw Hill.

3   Awarded by Business Ethics for service to seven stakeholder groups.

4   From The Forum for People Performance Management and Measurement, Northwestern University.

5   SouthWest has carried out in-depth research as to what drives customer satisfaction in the airline industry. The result was on-time flights, friendly service and low prices.

6   Howard Schultz (1997). *Pour Your Heart Into It.* Hyperion, 244.

5 Living the dream

He who has a 'why' to live, can bear with almost any 'how'.

FRIEDRICH NIETZSCHE (1844–1900)

It is one thing to have a dream; it is quite another to live up to that dream every day. That takes discipline, and that is often where strategy fails. While everyone is happy to spend two days discussing the future of the company, back at work they forget to focus on the set objectives, reinforcing them through their daily behavior and actions. As a result, employees look at their leaders and think 'If he doesn't care if I go all over the place, why should I?' 'If there are so many contradictions, how can I be clear?'

Discipline applies to every activity. If you decide to practice a dangerous sport, for example, you have to have the discipline to check your equipment before you climb or dive. If you fly a plane, you have to discipline yourself, even if you have flown that plane 25 or 25,000 times, to go through the check-list of what it takes for a plane to take off, fly and land safely. As such, discipline has nothing to do with creativity or personality traits, but everything to do with achieving what you set out to do.

This was brought home very powerfully by a mountaineering tragedy. On 10 May 1996, eight people died on Mount Everest, including world-renowned guides Scott Fischer and Rob Hall. Rob Hall was the owner and founder of Adventure Consultants, and Scott Fischer owned Mountain Madness. Both were seasoned guides with many trips to the Everest under their belts. In 1996, for the first time, the two men competed for publicity for their individual businesses. The one that got the most people to the top would win.

Mistakes were made on both sides that led to the fatal results: Scott left his clients to take down a friend suffering from altitude sickness, Rob broke his two o'clock turn-around time to take a second-time-round client to the top, and paths that should have been roped had to be arranged at the last minute.[1] The common thread of all of these errors, compounded by impending bad weather, was an appalling lack of discipline: the guides broke the rules they themselves had set, and the clients did not stand up to question their behavior (compliance rather than commitment).

Discipline is critical because it breeds consistency. It is the daily demonstration of focus around something you have decided to do. Having discipline means that whatever you say, whatever you do, wherever you are, whatever you push for – on a daily basis – has to be consistent with what you defined as your long-term goal.

the daily demonstration of focus around something you have decided to do

We believe that good execution can only happen through relentless individual and corporate discipline. It is the discipline demonstrated by the leaders of the company that matters. By leaders we mean anyone who has followers inside the company – which means more than just senior management. Individual discipline is exercised through a number of means, including the symbols and signals displayed by all those who have a leadership role in the company. It is critical that these be carefully thought through for it is through the symbols and signals that you exhibit that employees will decide whether to follow you or not.

Corporate discipline looks at how to deal with initiatives, making sure that they build on each other and that the company does not suffer from initiative fatigue. Finally, we consider how to stay in touch with reality, asking the right questions rather than protecting a dream that is derailing.

Personal discipline

You have a vision. Your board has bought into it. You have shared it with the organization. Now you need to make it **execution requires discipline from the organization and from its leaders** happen. This is the critical step – the point at which most management books stop and most companies stumble: execution. Execution requires discipline from the organization and from its leaders.

But how do you demonstrate personal discipline?

The simple answer is through signals and symbols. These are concrete translations of behavior that flag what you consider as important. They help you focus (see Figure 5.1). Below we define what we mean by symbols and signals and give examples of some of the most important of these.

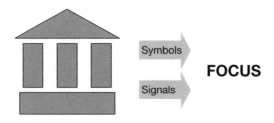

Figure 5.1 Symbols and signals as a means of focusing

A symbol is something you show your team. A signal is something you say or do, as it is heard or observed by your team. These are small, everyday actions and behaviors that the team can observe and think 'So he/she is serious about the vision. I can see it being carried out on a daily basis!' For example, if one of the pillars of your house focuses on the importance of customer relationships, and you never spend time with customers, never ask your team for information about your clients, or never visit any of your customers, there is no reason for your team to believe what you claim. To exercise discipline, and if customers really are key to achieving your vision, then you must spend time with them.

It is not easy to choose what to spend time on – there are only 24 hours in a day, so the amount of time you can spend with your customers is limited. That is why you need to think carefully about what you really think is important to your business and where you want to spend your time.

When Robert-Louis Dreyfuss became the CEO of adidas, the vision was rewritten to read 'best sports brand in the world' (see Chapter 2). As a result, Dreyfuss spent most of his time on managing the brand and on new products/innovation. For Dreyfuss, these were the two most critical signals when it came to becoming 'best sports brand'. His involvement in those two areas sent a far more powerful message than a long speech would have. As for symbols, he imposed English as the corporate language (worldwide), even though the headquarters were based in Germany and he himself did not speak English fluently.

Corporate semaphore

There are different types of symbols and signals, and which ones you use will depend on your style and on the company.

Issues

The first of these is the issues you choose to tackle. As executives, we delegate some issues and we want to be involved in others. The issues we choose to become involved in say a lot about what we consider important. Involvement can take different forms: it can be about problem definition, objective setting, options generation and evaluation, choice and implementation. If your strategy as a retailer is to be the cheapest, then you need to go to competing supermarkets, check the price of their products and confront your team if their products are cheaper than yours. That's a perfect signal. It is not about creativity but it does mean

> **the issues we choose to become involved in say a lot about what we consider important**

that you need to take the time to look through your competitors' shelves and confront your team. And if you do this relentlessly, slowly everyone on your team will be looking for low-cost, low-price items to put into the stores. If you don't look at these things, these 'details,' your vision is not likely to happen.

In Table 5.1, make a list of the issues you are currently involved in, with the type of involvement and the time spent on each. Does this list tell you that you are involved in the issues you should be involved in to make the vision happen, or are you sending the wrong signals? In the second column, add how you want to shift.

Table 5.1 Current issues

Issues	Type of involvement		Time spent	
Current	Today	Tomorrow	Today	Tomorrow
New				

Language

Language is mostly about terminology and a careful choice of words. For example, there is a difference between using the words 'customer complaint' or 'customer sufferings'. If you use the words 'customer sufferings' you are implying that every complaint is bad for the customer, while 'customer complaint' can be written off under the assumption that there are always people who will find fault, however perfect our products or services are. This means that if customer satisfaction is an essential part of achieving your vision, you may want to revisit the language you use and encourage the entire organization to change its vocabulary.

There are other concrete examples of how language is used/misused when aligned with the vision of the organization: cross-selling versus cross-buying (cross-selling is pushing another product on the customer. Cross-buying is helping the customer buy more of your products and services, because you provide additional value); headquarters versus service/support center (headquarters implies 'I'm the head, you are the legs').

Questions

How you ask questions also sends signals. For example, by always asking your employees the question, 'Is there another way?' you demonstrate that you value creativity. In the service industry, the priority is the company's clients, therefore, calling your staff into meetings with you, interrupting them during moments that should be dedicated to client interaction, sends the wrong signal. But not doing so requires discipline – it is easier to interrupt and get an answer right away than to wait until your staff can get back to you.

Interactions

Interactions are about whom you meet with first when you go to an office – is it the finance director or the head of R&D? And what does it signal when you meet one rather than the other more often? For example, if you are in the hotel business and you spend all of your time with the financial controller and are never seen in the kitchens, your employees will very quickly conclude that the financial position of the company is more important than the food served to the clients.

At Grand Optical, the top management team always visited the toilets before they looked at the store – there is no point in corporate talk about respect for employees if their workspace is derelict and dirty. They also

checked the training logbook and noted how many of a store's employees had gone to training courses beyond the induction course. This type
of information provided insight into the skill base of a store team as
well as turnover (all the employees are new and therefore there has
been no time for more advanced training) and about the store manager
– were training needs ignored because he or she believed it to be a
waste of time? In both cases, demonstrating
differentiation through interest in how well the store manager invests
service is key to the in his other staff reinforces the message that
company's retail differentiation through service is key to the
strategy company's retail strategy.

Interaction is also about the types of questions you ask: for example,
when an employee comes up with an idea, your first question might be,
'What will it do for the customer?', or it could be 'How much will it
cost?' The first signals your commitment to better service, the second
signals your interest in cost reduction. Not exactly the same thing is it?
Your questions must always support what is important for you, and
these questions should always be the same. Relentlessly.

Physical settings

Physical settings are mostly about symbols. Typically, by walking into
the office of a CEO, you can see what is important to them and how they
function. Physical settings are about what you put on your wall, your
desk, or in the company cafeteria. For example, putting expensive art
work on the walls of your company sends a different signal to that sent
by putting up photos of employees! Where the company is located is
also an important symbol.

In the support center (and NOT headquarters) of GrandVision (800
optical stores in the world), there is a 25 metre-long wall that leads to
the company cafeteria. Along the wall are pictures of every single store
and its store manager. The wall is called the 'Wall of Fame'. This sends
strong signals about several things: the fast growth of the company, the
importance of the store managers, and the importance of the field to the
people in the central structure.

At Euro Disney, to demonstrate the new behavior of the 'us' to all cast members, the HR team under the leadership of its director, picked up axes and broke down the poles placed on the parking spots of the cast members' main parking lot on which one could read 'Reserved for senior management'. This had a much more powerful effect that countless speeches on the importance of team work, team spirit, and so on.

Meetings and team composition

The people who are invited to participate in meetings are a far more important signal than the title of the meeting – who is involved says a lot about what you want to achieve, both during the meetings and after. This includes what goes on the agenda, the topics discussed and what is reported in the meeting minutes. Once again, if you say your clients are important but they are never on your agenda, it sends the wrong message. At Châteauform, every individual is asked to fill in an 'Astonishment Report' listing what they found positive or negative in the course of their first month with the company. This keeps everyone on their toes and provides many ideas for improvements and innovations. The company also runs four innovation labs per year, allowing different sites to present experiments and suggest innovations and improvements for the client. This has gone from new corkscrews or more silent vacuum cleaners to new architectural designs for the wellness centers. These two elements, among others, reinforce the company's commitment to service excellence and to constant innovation.

Deadlines

If deadlines are not respected when it comes to issues that are critical to the success of the vision, ask why. Also, stringent deadlines should be imposed on those issues that are critical to the execution of the vision.

Appointments

Who you appoint is a signal. If you say you believe in developing talent inside the company, and every time you hire a senior executive you hire him or her from outside, you are not consistent with your message, and you will loose your top-performing employees. Figure 5.2 summarizes the symbols and signals at your disposal to reinforce your vision and its implementation, as well as the questions you need to ask for each category.

Vision ➡

- **Presence:** where do you spend your time and with whom? Where are you seen?

- **Issues tackled:** what topics do you spend more time on? What ideas do you promote relentlessly? What issues do you celebrate? What deadlines are more stringent?

- **Language used:** what words do you use most frequently?

- **Interactions:** who do you see? What questions do you ask? How do you push on particular topics? What do you celebrate? What do you say in public speeches? Who do you celebrate?

- **Physical settings:** what does your office (space, desk, walls, furniture), car, dress, business card, title say? Where are you located?

- **Coordination meetings:** who do you involve? Who gets to tackle what? What subjects are discussed? In what order? What do the minutes say?

- **Appointments:** who do you promote? What do they represent to others? What is the image? Who do you celebrate?

Figure 5.2 The different manifestations of signals and symbols

Hewlett Packard (HP) is a good example of a company that thinks carefully about symbols and signals. This is easily demonstrated using the company's value system. HP lists seven values as being critical to their business success: a passion for the customer; trust and respect for everybody; management by contribution and not by attribution; speed of action and flexibility; innovation that sells, not innovation that is artistic and overpriced; teamwork and integrity.

The company does not run an induction program – you go straight to your job. So how do employees learn these values? For one, the recruitment process is very thorough, with both sides checking for fit, and HP in particular looking for a demonstration of those values in potential employees. Candidates who do not 'fit in' will tend to opt out at this stage.

The fact that there is no induction program also supports two of the company's values: management by contribution – you are recognized for your contribution and not for your title; and speed of action and flexibility – you are expected to start contributing immediately and making your own place in the sun. This internal job market means that it is up to you to get others to recognize your talents.

Another symbol is relayed by the fact that there are no visible signs of hierarchy. For instance, there is no parking allocated to management and open space applies to everyone – there are no corner offices. This contributes to building a culture of trust, respect and equality.

Job posting is another example. When a position becomes vacant, it is posted on the intranet, and if you choose to take that job you leave immediately. You don't stay three months. If you feel you can contribute more elsewhere, there is no point in keeping you in your current job.

By contrast, in banking, you rarely find people who began their careers in the subsidiaries, working at the desks! What signal does this send as to the importance of customer interface, customer service?

Celebrating

What you celebrate should be directly linked to your vision. You may, for instance, choose to link rewards to the different pillars of the vision, and to the desired behaviors. Rewards should happen on a yearly basis and should be consistent – changing the things you reward is once again a lack of consistency.

At Châteauform, there are seven awards every year that correspond to those behaviors that have been defined as supporting the vision. These are: love of the client; continuous learning; loyalty, integrity, honesty; contribution not attribution; entrepreneurial, family spirit and performance. In addition, the employees who stay are valued, and given a reward for 5, 10 and 20 years of loyalty.

Below you will find two tables that will help you identify what you should do more of and less of in terms of symbol and signals. Table 5.2 suggests listing a few key ways on which to focus in the future. Which ones are important for you to focus on?

Table 5.2 Determining key symbols and signals

Focus for the future	Are they key to achieving our vision? (tick)	Ideal symbol or signal		
		1	2	3
Speed	❑			
Innovation	❑			
Brand	❑			
Cost	❑			
Internationalization	❑			
...				

Next, look at what you do today in greater detail, and decide what you should reinforce or eliminate (Table 5.3).

Table 5.3 Do you have the right mix?

Symbols and Signals	My current symbols and signals	New/future signals and symbols	Which ones should I eliminate?
Presence			
Language			
Questions			
Issues			
Meetings			
Celebrations			
Appointments			
Deadlines			

Discipline in an organization is not only about how individuals behave, and what symbols and signals they uphold. It is also about how the organization behaves as a whole – i.e. corporate discipline. This is what we will be looking into next.

> **discipline in an organization is not only about how individuals behave, and what symbols and signals they uphold**

Corporate discipline

Initiatives as walls: one brick at a time, building on one another

When Daimler merged with Chrysler in October 1998 the new group launched 50 initiatives. Two years later, 50 per cent of these had been dropped, changed or replaced with something else.[2] The post-merger financial results were not very good either. Yet the company was not the first or even the only large corporation to suffer from initiatives overload.

Many companies suffer from initiative fatigue – the big, expensive corporate initiatives that require important commitment both in terms of resources (money and people) and in terms of time. The fatigue is not a result of the initiatives themselves but is directly linked to the fact that too many initiatives are launched simultaneously, without having seen the results of the previous ones, and without taking the time to take stock of whether one initiative worked before starting the next one. With time, these initiatives begin to be perceived as 'flavor of the year' 'flavor of the month', 'flavor of the day' by employees, and are no longer dealt with seriously.

The most effective approach to corporate initiatives is to use one initiative as a spring board for the next one. Too few top–down initiatives reinforce the next one with the previous one. Let us go back to our customer satisfaction example. Because you have stated that customer satisfaction is important to you, you choose to introduce a new customer satisfaction measure. And let us suppose that the second initiative in that area will be to train all of your employees on customer culture, customer philosophy, and customer service. So first you design a global survey around customer satisfaction and then you train everyone worldwide on customer satisfaction. Exercising discipline means that once you move on to the second initiative, you continue running regular customer satisfaction measures, and you transform this one-time training effort into a constant training program for new employees.

The house that Jack built

In the case of GE under the leadership of Jack Welch as CEO,[3] every corporate initiative built on the previous one, was launched one at a time and was sustained after the next one was launched. There was also an evolution in the types of initiatives pursued: over the course of 20 years, the initiatives that were launched shifted from the 'hard to soft', and from the systemic to the behavioral. The early initiatives supported the transformation of the company and its vision. They were very systemic and process-oriented, while the later ones were more behavioral or people-oriented. The early ones set the scene, the later ones allowed the company to keep moving forward, as depicted in Figure 5.3.

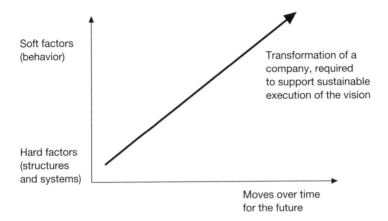

Figure 5.3 Initiatives

The resources put forward to support the initiatives were significant ('put your money where your mouth is' is a very powerful signal). To add clout to the importance of the initiatives, each one was run by a 'champion' – always a senior executive reporting directly to Jack Welch.

> **'put your money where your mouth is' is a very powerful signal**

A CEO-backed initiative definitely adds weight to the importance of what must be accomplished. The ability to say 'we spoke about this in our meeting yesterday' sends a signal about the importance of the initiative. This systematic approach to initiatives was set in place as the result of a vision expressed early on in the game: 'Be No. 1 or No. 2, if not: fix, close, sell.'

Table 5.4 gives some examples of the initiatives run over the course of Welch's tenure.

With time, these initiatives moved from hard to soft, from products, processes and the basic working of the company to softer factors such as culture and leadership. But throughout this 20-year span, Welch managed to enforce discipline and continuity of each initiative. And when you exercise discipline and continuity in your initiatives, they slowly become part of the fabric of the company. Over those 20 years, Welch radically transformed the company and its culture.

> **when you exercise discipline and continuity in your initiatives, they slowly become part of the fabric of the company**

Table 5.4 Initiatives run over the course of Jack Welch's tenure at GE

Moves for the future	Initiatives on hard factors (hardware)	Initiatives on soft factors (software)
1981	No. 1, or No. 2 (fix, close or sell)	
1983	Three circles: business categorized as core, high tech or services	
	Destaffing. 50% reduction in the 200-strong strategic planning group.	
	5-page strategy play book (real-time planning) Budgeting focused on external factors	
1985	Down from 9 to 4 hierarchical levels	
1988		Work out. 3-day sessions where groups of 40 to 100 employees spoke openly about their businesses and what could be improved. On the third day, the bosses were presented with initiatives and requests which they had to respond to immediately
		Best practices. Learning from other companies. Became part of the work out agenda and training

Table 5.4 *Continued*

Moves for the future	Initiatives on hard factors (hardware)	Initiatives on soft factors (software)
1989	Over the period since 1980 headcount dropped from 404,000 to 292,000	
1990s	Global thrust to support growth	
		Using HR to support culture change. Leadership development. Career maps. Intensive use of Crotonville. Importance of values Boundaryless behavior. Stretch
	Move away from industrial products to services. Encouraged all businesses to explore service-based growth opportunities	
1996	Six Sigma. Zero Defect. Six Sigma quality levels to be reached by 2000	
1997	20 service-related acquisitions. By end of decade, services would represent $\frac{2}{3}$ of revenue	
		Focus on A players and the the three 'E's of energy, energizing others and edge for GE leaders

The umbrella approach

As an alternative to launching a major corporate initiative every year, building on the previous one, some companies use the umbrella approach. These companies find it useful to create an umbrella initiative under which all other initiatives will have to fall. The electronics retailer Best Buy uses this approach. In May 2003 faced with steep competition and the introduction of more complex products it launched an overarching Customer Centricity initiative. This initiative encompassed all other initiatives – for example, cost-saving measures were taken in other parts of the business in order to fund customer centricity measures. (We will discuss Best Buy in greater detail in the next chapter.)

Tetra Pak, leader in packaging systems for the dairy and soft drinks industry, launched the 'win back' initiative in 2000 when it realized that customers were growing dissatisfied with their service level. This 'win back' was aimed at eliminating all customer frustration and led to a quasi total disappearance of customer complaints on efficiency, improvement in customer's line efficiency from 88 per cent to 94 per cent, and reduction in machine down-time from 6 hours to 1.5 hours per incident.[4]

Look at all your company initiatives and ask yourself the following questions.

- ❖ Do our current initiatives build on what was done before?
- ❖ Or do they tend to ignore what worked before?
- ❖ Do all projects and micro top–down initiatives fall under an umbrella thrust or do all initiatives tend to have a life of their own?
- ❖ Can we regroup all initiatives under an umbrella initiative?
- ❖ If so, can we justify all existing ones or should we eliminate some? Which ones?

The problem with the dream and the organization becoming so closely knit is that you run the risk of losing touch with reality, spinning out of reality in a world of your fabrication. This is what we will look at next.

Staying in touch

Institutionalized discipline is about being in touch with the right things. Pursuing intimate knowledge of the business is closely linked to discipline. Often as a company grows larger, its senior executives lose touch with the reality of the front line. Yet there are many ways in which you can stay in touch. Euro Disney runs an annual commitment called 'Showtime' – for four days, every executive, independent of hierarchical level, has to go back into the park and sell hotdogs or sweep the floor.

Another way of staying in touch with your business is to use your products and services as a normal customer would, and not go through a special channel. It is much easier if you are, say, the CEO of BMW, to call your secretary and say, 'I want a new car' and have it delivered to your house. It takes greater discipline to go to a garage, incognito, and buy your new car. But this approach will tell you about the experience your customers go through, the issue of 'just-in-time', the fact that you cannot get a car, the issue of consistency of the brand, the cost in the distribution channel. You learn something that the reports and the key performance indicators (KPIs) cannot tell you.

You can also consciously select people from different backgrounds. This will give you a different set of outlooks on reality. This is what the CEO of British Petroleum, John Brown did when he hired a team of 24-year-old students to tell him about the aspirations of their generation for the future. He was willing to meet them on their grounds, listen to them, and much of the last BP campaign on renewable energy came out of those discussions with a youth he originally knew nothing of.

selecting people from different backgrounds will give you a different set of outlooks on reality

Obviously, intimate knowledge of how your customers think and behave is an essential part of staying in touch with reality. Run focus groups – but make sure you attend them personally; ask your customers what types of solutions they are interested in – basically, put yourself in their shoes. At COOP, one of the two largest Swiss general merchandise retailers, the CEO and all board members perform bi-monthly store tours and checks. They report their findings back at every board meeting.

A good example of putting yourself in your customers' shoes is the cancellation policies of hotels with regard to seminars. Every hotel applies a cancellation fee against companies who either cancel a booking for a seminar or change the number of participants attending. These policies are there to 'protect the business' irrespective of the concerns of the client. Cancellation fees usually include approximately 50 per cent of the total amount up to 30 days prior to the seminar, an additional 30 per cent when cancelled 10–15 days prior to the date and 100 per cent when the cancellation occurs within 48 hours of the given date.

In most cases, companies cancel or postpone at very short notice, and the person in charge of booking, usually the assistant to the seminar leader, is blamed for the cost of the cancellation or postponement. Arguments fly back and forth, and depending on the clout of the customer, the hotel may waive its fee or accept being recognized as inflexible and anti-business. When Châteauform entered the seminar business, it realized that the traditional cancellation policies went against the company's differentiation.[5] So it ran focus groups to decide how to avoid what lead to customer irritation and ill-will. The purpose was to find a solution that would be acceptable to clients, while being positive for Châteauform's image. Different options were suggested and the one retained by customers involved a 5 per cent application processing fee, to be charged only if the seminar was cancelled, with no set time limit; and also the possibility of postponing a seminar over a six-month period with no additional cost. The workshops were run with actual clients, some of which had had to cancel in the past and others who had never cancelled. These clients were the ones that chose the final solution.

staying in touch with your business helps you stay on track
Putting yourself in your customers' shoes, staying in touch with your business helps you stay on track, and yet sometimes the vision still does not seem to happen. In Chapter 6 we will consider in greater detail how rules, regulations and the existence of a clandestine culture can destroy the implementation of a vision.

... and following through

Staying in touch is not just linked to personal discipline but also to institutionalized practices. Some of these have been described already:

❖ 'show time' for every executive on the front line;

❖ put yourself in the shoes of your customers;

❖ 'astonishment reports' for all new employees;

❖ every executive introduces the vision to new employees during the induction programs;

❖ all qualitative customer research is attended by senior executives;

❖ all senior executives must buy company products like normal customers;

❖ visits to sites, call centers, etc. are organized on a systematic basis for all senior executives.

Many other ways exist to institutionalize staying in touch. At one 20,000-strong company, the CEO invites, on a monthly basis, employees to a give-and-take, question-and-answers breakfast. In another company, all leaders must spend 20 per cent of their time in the training sessions of the corporate university. Finally, in another group, the number of hierarchical levels has been fixed to three, with everyone having to fit into those three levels.

There will never be enough investment made on staying in touch. What has your organization institutionalized to promote, with discipline, the implementation of your vision? What else can you do?

Turning ideas into action

Beyond staying in touch and creating initiatives that build on one another, or creating umbrella initiatives under which all others **organizational discipline is about turning ideas into action** must fall, organizational discipline is also about turning ideas into action.

How many times do we leave a meeting with the impression that great ideas were discussed but that nothing will happen? It can be that no-one was appointed to take the idea forward. Or that the ideas were not tested against current reality to see what could be easily implemented and what would be difficult. Or it could be that there wasn't even a summary of the ideas generated. How often do we receive reports (market, customer research, indicators), that we read, summarize, analyze, and then ... continue with business as usual? How often do we see an idea outside our own organization, or in another part of the organization, and lack the discipline to transfer this idea to our own organization or across boundaries within the organization?

These are all examples of lack of discipline in an institutionalized approach to turning ideas into actions. Below is a list of questions that can help you avoid the traps.

- ❖ Does every idea have an owner who can turn it into action?
- ❖ Do we systematically leave a meeting in which a report was presented (whether external or internal) with a list of actions to be taken?
- ❖ If we see something good in one part of the organization, do we systematically disseminate it across the organization through an organized process (annual show, share-and-learn seminars, intranet, personal note sent to x, y, z ... ?

Summary

Successful execution is heavily dependant on individual and corporate discipline. Discipline is important because its breeds consistency and focus. Everything you do, say, ask or inspect has to be consistent with your vision.

Individual discipline is expressed through symbols and signals. These are concrete translations of behavior that flag what you consider as important.

A symbol is something you show your team.

A signal is something you say or do.

Individual discipline is expressed through different media, including the words you use (customer complaint versus customer suffering), your location, who gets invited to meetings, how well deadlines are respected, whom you appoint (and from where) to senior positions and what you celebrate.

Corporate discipline is primarily about the way in which you handle initiatives. Avoid initiative fatigue and make sure that each initiative builds on the previous one. Also think about building umbrella initiatives under which all others fall.

Staying in touch with the reality of the business is closely linked to discipline. Often, as a company grows larger, its senior executives lose touch with the reality of the front line. Some ways of staying in touch include using your products as your customers would, sending senior executives back to the field, selecting people with diverse backgrounds and putting yourself in the shoes of your customers.

Finally, it is important to have an institutionalized process for turning ideas into action.

NOTES TO CHAPTER 5

1 Jon Krakauer (1998). *Into Thin Air: A Personal Account of the Mt. Everest Disaster* (Anchor, repr. 1999).
Anatoli Boukreev and G. Weston DeWalk (1998). *The Climb: Tragic Ambitions on Everest* (St Martin's Paperbacks).
Michael A. Roberto and Gina M. Carioggia (2003). Mount Everest 1–1 1996. Harvard business school case study, 9-303-061.

2 Daimler Chrysler Headline (2002). Newsletter for management, 18, 11 October.

3 Christopher A. Bartlett and M. Wozny (1999). GE's two-decade transformation: Jack Welch's leadership, Harvard Business School case study no. 399–150.

4 Kamran Kashani (2002). Tetra Pak (D): Results achieved (and the remaining issues). IMD case study. IMD-5-0607.

5 It originally had a similar cancellation policy to that of hotels: 70 per cent 15 days prior to the start date, 90 per cent for 15 days or less. This was applied quite strictly since, contrary to standard hotels, the client could not be replaced that easily in a short time-frame.

6 Built to dream ... with open eyes

Hell, there are no rules here – we're trying to accomplish something. THOMAS A. EDISON

In this chapter we look at how organizational structures either help or hinder the execution of the vision.

Countless books have been published on structure, and it would be foolish to try and summarize them here. Instead, we will look at different mechanisms that have important implications for the execution of the vision. These include the definition of roles and responsibilities – to ensure that alignment around the vision occurs, the appointment of champions – to share and execute the vision, and the degree of coordination and cooperation across the business – to ensure that everyone is going in the same direction. These go in parallel with the need to replace rigid structures with principles and processes.

We then move on to look at how to measure progress and how to use incentives as a tool for motivating teams to make the vision happen. We follow with rewards, as these are closely linked to measurement. Finally, we look at the everyday behaviors that prevent a vision from happening.

Supporting the vision

To a large extent, the successful implementation of a vision depends on having an organizational design that supports its execution. The two must be aligned. This includes everything from how departments are organized, and who is responsible for what, to reporting relationships and coordination mechanisms. Often, you will need to revisit at least part of the company's organizational design to implement your vision.

the successful implementation of a vision depends on having an organizational design that supports the execution of the vision

A case in point is the insurance industry. Insurance companies all deal with the same challenge: sell more than two insurance policies per individual. The current ratio is on average 1.8 policies per person, whereas customers typically have eight to ten policies. So why is it so difficult to sell more than two policies per individual? There could be several reasons for this:

❖ Customers do not want to put all of their eggs in the same basket. This reason does not seem to be realistic, given the A ratings of most insurance companies.

❖ Lack of ability – insurance companies don't know how to 'cross-sell', i.e. encourage customers who already have one or two policies with the company to buy others. Given the lucrative remuneration of most insurance agents and brokers (commission on the insurance premium) this reason does not hold water either.

The reasons are actually the result of a structural legacy.

❖ The IT legacy is by contract, or by policy, not by person, so there is no knowledge-sharing about how many contracts a person may have with the company and what else they might be sold.

❖ The market structure of insurance companies is typically around products rather than by client segments.

❖ The risk of each client – and thus the price – is assessed by actuaries, and traditionally they assess risk types, not people within their specific context.

The AXA insurance group changed its US structure to address this issue. They understood that the legacy structure was getting in the way of additional revenue, and so began their transformation with the company's marketing and customer relations functions.

Traditionally, the company's relationship marketing group was organized around marketing tactics, not customers. Market research, recognized as the source of customer insight, and therefore the area that should drive strategy and tactics, was one of nine areas (which included alliances, advertising, sports marketing or local market development). In addition, research focused primarily on products and distribution, much less on specific customer segments. Figure 6.1 shows the organizational chart as it existed at the time.

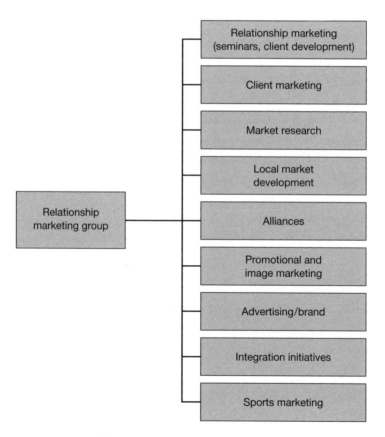

Figure 6.1 AXA's marketing structure up to 2005

As a result of this observation, in 2005 AXA completely redesigned its marketing and customer relationship functions to center primarily on specific customer segments (Figure 6.2).

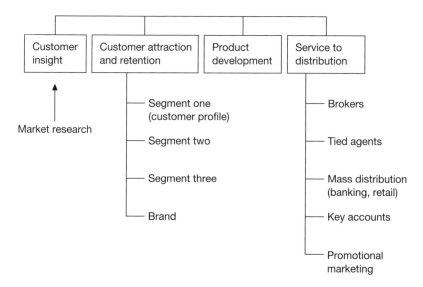

Figure 6.2 AXA's revised organizational structure, focusing on customer segments rather than products

The new vision was clearly more client-focused and described the 'one-stop shop' approach that became the base of their phenomenal success.

> Financial Protection involves offering our customers – individuals as well as small, mid-size and large businesses – a wide range of products and services that meet their insurance, protection, savings, retirement and financial planning needs throughout their lives, enabling them to be life confident.[1]

As this example demonstrates, one of the first ways to make the vision happen is to reshuffle the organizational structure.

one of the first ways to make the vision happen is to reshuffle the organizational structure

If the vision calls for customer centricity, then responsibilities for marketing by customer segments and customer insight must feature prominently in the organizational structure. When Best Buy, introduced customer centricity, it appointed five customer segments executives responsible for providing the products and services that went with each of those high potential segments. This was a key departure from the structure of the past in which key responsibilities for store operations where determined by product category (brown goods, electronics, software, etc.) rather than by customer segments.

If the vision calls instead for leadership in quality (or innovation, or another dimension) then once again the critical roles and responsibilities must be given a prominent place at the highest possible level in the hierarchy. When GE embarked on Six Sigma, 5,000 people were trained to become 'black belts' and given the responsibility of facilitating in any way possible the zero defect target.

If the vision calls for something broader, for example 'Achieve all synergies by 2006', then key projects must be identified, project leaders and project teams appointed. These teams will then suggest the best way of making the synergies happen. The teams must not only have the authority to make recommendations (nice to have but not enough), but also the power to execute the necessary change, through their teams, and also by reporting to a 'synergy' steering committee, able to commit and allocate resources and take risks.

The dream team

In the previous chapter we discussed the importance of corporate initiatives, built one at a time and building on each other. This approach requires appointing champions who will ensure that the initiatives happen. One obvious and powerful way is to appoint executives who will be responsible for the execution of each of the key ways expressed in the vision. For example, when GE decided to implement total quality, Jack Welch appointed a Six Sigma champion. He did the same thing for his Work Out, global (boundary-less) or best practice initiatives.

Champions are a good way of signaling that the CEO supports a specific initiative, and a great way of making sure that it happens. Each champion is responsible for meeting targets and objectives that are specific to that initiative.

The issue with champions is twofold:

❖ How much clout will they have to make things happen?

❖ How will they get the organization to move forward?

The best way of addressing these questions is to appoint champions who are

❖ close to the top, reporting directly to the CEO

❖ seasoned enough in their accumulated experience to avoid power games, to be recognized as legitimate by line management, and with the necessary skills to get things done through people.

Being a champion requires

❖ a lot of traveling

❖ a lot of talking

❖ a lot of teaching

❖ a lot of pedagogy.

The champion who reports to the CEO or COO needs to be a seasoned executive, with a proven track record but with the rare ability *to do nothing* other than convince! Not easy for someone who has been successful doing and obtaining results through actions and decisions. The person needs to be able to inspire others, reinforcing the part of the vision which they have been appointed to champion, typically through a major corporate initiative.

Obviously a single senior champion is not good enough. That individual needs relays across the organization, something along the line of the 5,000 black belts mentioned earlier.

As part of their 'winning the hearts of Europe' vision, Euro Disney decided to increase the interaction between cast and guests. The initiative, called Disney Style, required that all 12,000 cast members have at least five interactions per day with five different guests. Understandingly, most cast members, for fear of having to deal with negative comments, or lacking the skills to interact (easier to run a ride than to do prep talk with a customer), were reluctant. The initiative, driven by the head of HR, was supported throughout the hotels and the park by 100 managers and team leaders. These champions discussed the 'why' of the initiative and provided support to those cast members who were reluctant to approach clients. Together, they thought through ways of approaching guests, and how to respond to negative criticism. In the course of a month, 1,200 cast members were ready to try the new approach ... and surprise, surprise – four out of five interactions turned out to be compliments (the interactions were recorded as a ways of improving quality through customer feedback). The initiative boosted morale and encouraged the drive to win the hearts of Europe ... .

Whereas specific champions can be appointed to herald a specific initiative, it remains important that the primary champions are those who contributed to its expression, typically the senior management team, including the CEO, direct reports and senior line management.

Any member of the executive who, once the vision has been defined, does not champion it, should be asked to leave. While it is one thing to argue, disagree, discuss before the dream is defined and the key ways of achieving it are spelt out, it is another thing to opt out once the decisions have been taken. It is not acceptable not to embrace the vision wholeheartedly – at least not until it has been proven wrong – something which does not happen overnight.

> **it is one thing to argue, disagree, discuss before the dream is defined, it is another thing to opt out once the decisions have been taken**

Role casting

The ways roles and responsibilities are defined and allocated send clear signals about what is important to you or not. Going back to our GE example, Welch's Work Out initiative (the three-day meetings in which employees could express openly their suggestions for the business, and bosses had to veto or agree to these initiatives on the spot) was more than a means of increasing productivity. It changed the nature of management roles and responsibilities; creating a safe environment in which employees at all levels were encouraged to question and challenge decisions, and suggest new ways of doing things. Senior managers were encouraged to listen and to shift to a participative management style that was far from the traditional top–down role.

In the late 1970s, the consulting firm McKinsey & Company was feeling the heat of increasing competition from upstarts such as BCG and the growing expectations from increasingly sophisticated clients.[2] At the time, the company was organized around locally based client relationship consulting. McKinsey's managing director, Ron Daniel, realized that the company had to become more specialized and change its structure. As a result, he reorganized the firm around global, industry-based client segments (banking, consumer goods, industrial goods, etc.). He also encouraged knowledge sharing and knowledge codification in functional areas such as strategy, marketing and organizational design. He created 15 virtual centers of competence codifying management expertise. The firm had to work hard to support the idea that it wasn't only the size of one's client base that mattered, but that functional specialists were just as important. (In the words of one team member, 'Would you like your brain surgery done by a general practitioner?')[2]

The knowledge-based structure that ensued is the one that exists today, earning McKinsey its 'thought leader' reputation. To make it happen, senior consultants had to reallocate roles and responsibilities, ensuring that both client relationships and knowledge management were equally respected. One way of doing this was to make it clear that a consultant could make a career in the firm by being a specialist. Another was to appoint highly regarded and respected senior consultants in knowledge generation and management roles.

Looking at the key responsibilities developed recently in an organization says a lot about whether the vision has a good chance of being implemented, as do the titles and responsibilities of the CEO's direct reports. Making the vision happen is a lot more difficult if the job descriptions of senior management do not match the new orientation!

All together now

In our complex, global, interconnected world, cooperation has to a large extent replaced competition. Increasingly, suppliers, customers and competitors work together. They build common internet marketplaces and industry platforms. In parallel, companies are increasingly moving from a control structure to a coordination structure. This is done through the use of cross-boundary spanners, virtual teams, and cross-functional teams. In this context, the question is how do headquarters add value? And in a multibusiness context, what is the value in coordination? Why do it?

cooperation has to a large extent replaced competition

A good example of how headquarters can add value is the French conglomerate Pinault Printemps Redoute (PPR). The company employs 81,000 people and posted revenue of €17.8 billion in 2005. They were the leading retail group in Europe (with companies like FNAC, Conforama, Redcats, Printemps, etc.) and third globally in the luxury goods industry (they own the Gucci group).[3] The conglomerate ran both business-to-business (B2B) operations and business-to-consumer (B2C) operations through its diverse group of businesses. As a result of this diversity, the balance between central control and company autonomy had always been a delicate issue. In the words of the president of one of the businesses,

> It's like a big federation where we share common qualitative values and common quantitative objectives.[4]

The presidents of each business were free to run their company as they saw fit, and they had full operational responsibility. In their own words, they combined decentralized management with pooled resources and know-how. Operational freedom was balanced with tight financial planning. The presidents met with the heads of the PPR group every year to agree on strategic plans and budget. They then met on a monthly basis to review performance versus objectives. The group actively encouraged internal mobility and cross-company career development. They published a group-wide monthly magazine that posted all of the available group positions. They also capitalized on the similarities between the different groups – they were all distribution companies and none of them manufacture anything.

To increase cooperation and coordination between the different businesses, headquarters designed a common set of values. These were:

- ❖ seeing clearly
- ❖ speaking honestly
- ❖ mastering complexity
- ❖ having a sense of time
- ❖ taking ambition to the highest level
- ❖ succeeding together.

But this was not enough – PPR felt the need to increase the synergies between the distribution businesses, with a vision to:

- ❖ increasing sales outside France (while 70 per cent of the groups sales were made in France in 1994, this number had already dropped to 50 per cent by 1999)
- ❖ grow from a €19 billion business in 2000 to €27 billion by 2003.

Immediately, headquarters appointed two champions who would lead the worldwide efforts.

- ❖ One champion was in charge of looking at pooling resources to reduce costs such as buying material (typical sourcing economies) but also more sophisticated approaches to pooling, such as sharing customer data across the groups of companies. A person buying a book at FNAC could also be buying clothes at the Printemps department store.

❖ The second champion was in charge of the development of internet retailing, with the minimum requirement being to share a common platform.

These decisions were conscious decisions around increasing coordination. They achieved one of the key objectives a headquarter likes to have: add corporate value, which is what we called corporate advantage in Chapter 2.

Corporate advantage in the case of a retail/luxury group such as PPR could happen in several ways:

❖ Boost business performance: for instance, through management processes, or best-practice-sharing (organized by headquarters).

❖ Boost 'relatedness': synergies are created in buying, in sharing customer data, and in building common platforms.
Implementing these synergies requires corporate champions.

How big?

Corporate headquarters can thus add value and contribute to achieving the vision if their size, role and responsibilities fit the intended strategic direction.

The biggest hurdle to delivering corporate advantage is deciding on what coordination mechanisms to use, which in turn is linked to the level of added value the corporation hopes to achieve. This will have an influence on the size and role of the corporate headquarters. This can be illustrated using Figure 6.3.

the biggest hurdle to delivering corporate advantage is deciding on what coordination mechanisms to use

First, the size of the corporate centre will depend on the group's strategy. A *financial holding* will have smaller coordination needs than a *formula developer*. The great diversity of the businesses will mean that at best you can reproduce a management model (as with GE). The role of headquarters will primarily be to sponsor key initiatives that have corporate-wide effects (such as Six Sigma) and to develop the common management model that underlines the vision and its supporting behaviors (which is why GE's corporate university has always been a key function of the role of headquarters). An *international operator* will coordinate only some specific functions, such as IT or marketing. A *formula developer*, will reproduce a similar business globally, and therefore your coordination needs, and the role of the headquarters, is greater. In this expanded role, headquarters need to formalize the formula, and replicate it with the necessary 'control' across the brand, the different operations and subsidiaries.

The size of the corporate centre is also linked to the degree of centralization and therefore the amount of coordination needed to run the

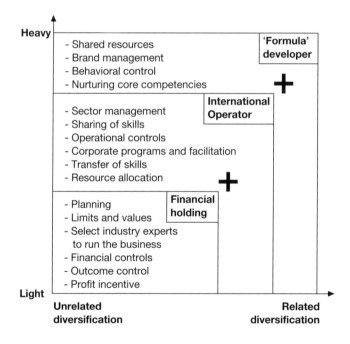

Figure 6.3 The size of the corporate center depends on the strategy chosen

the size of headquarters depends on the degree of centralization and coordination needed

businesses. Centralization is not only necessary with regard to 'control' but also to achieve synergies. A corporate vision that emphasizes synergies would most probably lead to a much more centralized structure than one which emphasizes the conquest of new markets (lighter headquarters with autonomous business units organized by geography. For example, when IBM needed to reinvent itself, its new CEO, Lou Gerstner changed the structure, responsibility and role of headquarters. One of his first actions was to get rid of the countless levels of bureaucracy that had built up over the years. He designed a new structure based on decentralized decision-making with a centralized strategy and a common customer focus aimed at creating a company that was market-driven and not process-driven. To do this the company was reorganized around global industry teams. He aligned the incentive programs to reward customer focus. Bonuses were linked to the overall performance of the company and not to specific divisions; and he worked on the culture of the company, which had become fatalistic: 'I want can-do people looking for short-term victories and long-term excitement.'[5]

Clearly, the type of mechanisms that you put in place depends on your vision and the role of headquarters in that vision – if your vision is to conquer new markets, the role of headquarters will be different from that in IBM's case, where customer focus across the whole organization was a priority. The type of mechanisms needed, depending on the degree of centralization, are shown in Figure 6.4.

These different approaches increase collaboration and cooperation without controlling heavily the way in which each individual business functions. The structure is seen as supporting the vision rather than as a hurdle to be overcome.

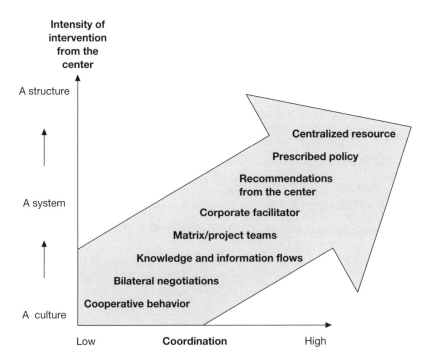

Figure 6.4 Coordination mechanisms depend on the degree of centralization

First principles

While structure can support the execution of a vision through the use of champions, the redefinition of roles and responsibilities and coordination mechanisms, it is sometimes not enough to make the vision happen. Why?

❖ Structures are sometimes too mechanistic.

❖ They pigeon-hole roles – for example, we use the word 'division' to name a strategic business unit but divisions 'divide' whereas vision aligns.

divisions 'divide' whereas vision aligns

As a result, some companies would rather use principles and processes than try to change the structure.

Think about the following elements of the customer philosophy of Federal Express:

❖ The customer is always right.

❖ Quality: a dollar spent on prevention is better than a dollar spent on correcting a mistake.

❖ We are never satisfied with what we do. We should do better, all the time.

❖ The customer should drive all of our decisions.

❖ What does not get measured does not progress.

Can these principles guide action and execution without changing the structure?

Think about some of the management principles of the French optics retailer GrandVision, illustrated with excerpts from their Management Principles Manual.[6]

❖ **Management by contribution, not attribution**

We prefer managers who contribute to the overall goals rather than those who manage by exclusive territories. We must allow someone from another function to give their view on our function, even if the final decision is ours.

❖ **We are all teachers**

It is our duty to pass on our knowledge. We should volunteer to be trainers and not refuse when asked.

❖ **Let's be transparent**

We want all of our associates to know why we do things in the way that we do them. An associate should refuse to perform a task if they don't know why they should be doing it.

❖ **The truth is in the field**

The truth is found where customers and associates are. Everyone should spend time in the stores. When recruited, everyone should visit the stores.

All associates have the right to tell their store manager, regional manager, managing director, president, what they think.

❖ **Making things work requires, most of the time, an attitude of 'just do it'.**

Meetings are costly and time consuming. They must therefore be conclusive, ending with personal and dated plans of action. (...)

❖ **We prefer managing by the principles of subsidiarity**

('you can do everything, except ... ') rather than by delegation ('You can do nothing except ... ').

❖ **The inverted pyramid: delegate upwards what you don't want**

If there is something that a level does not want to do because it interferes with taking care of the store team and the customers, it should be given to the next level up. In this way we are sure that stores spend most of their time with customers and associates!

Principles guide action better than structures do, if they are acknowledged and shared by everyone. Action in turn leads to making the dream happen within the deadline! Principles can also resist better to change in circumstances, and they weave the fabric of an organization that is bent on making things happen.

principles guide action better than structures do

Taking appropriate measures

There's an old saying 'People respect what you inspect.' As a leader you need to carefully select what you push for, and you should push for what contributes most to the vision. But do not micro-manage or get involved in the details. What is important is that you manage what is key. Discipline in this case is about always going back to the list of things you agreed on and then giving your team the freedom to implement.

For example, when Jacques meets the construction manager at Châteauform, he does not ask him about budget or quality issues, because those are areas of expertise best left to him. But he does ask him when the new site will open because that is key – if the site opening is delayed, customers (who book three to six months in advance) will not have a place to go to. And what matters to the business is the customer. It's about not getting involved in what is not key (as we mentioned earlier when discussing symbols and signals). Similarly, before meeting the director of operations it is important to read all of the customer feedback forms – if they reflect extraordinary customer satisfaction the team involved must be congratulated. If there is a problem it needs to be discussed with the director of operations. If even a small detail goes wrong, the story will be shared with everyone, sending the signal 'We care about our customers, and the devil is in the details.'

Plots and plans

We define a plan as a decision made today for tomorrow, which already disqualifies most plans made by companies, as

a plan is a decision made today for tomorrow

they tend to be forecasts rather than decisions. There are three types of plans that serve as sounding boards to measure progress: strategic plans, operational plans and budgets.

❖ A strategic plan (3–10 years) answers the two fundamental questions behind any business: what business(es) to be in because of their attractiveness to us and what competitive advantage to develop.

❖ An operational plan (2–5 years) outlines key operational decisions – these include marketing decisions, R&D, production, investments.

Both the strategic and operational plan should find their roots in the vision, and more specifically in the pillars of the house model. Remember that the title of each pillar represents a source of competitive advantage and the list of actions and milestones are the key elements that will be turned into detailed operating plans.

❖ The budget plan (one year) is about resource allocation. This includes how much you will spend on marketing, HR, new recruits, etc.

Bear in mind that a plan is only as good as its control mechanisms. Control allows us to assess whether the plan is on track or not, and if not, what needs to be done to get back on **a plan is only as good as its control mechanisms** track. Each plan should therefore carry with it a specific set of measurements, as shown in Figure 6.5.

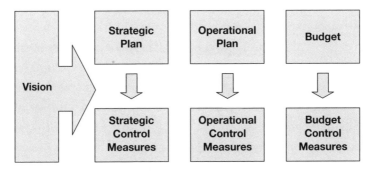

Figure 6.5 The vision plan

For budgets, it is best to look at the variance between what we set out to spend and what was actually spent, and ask

❖ Did we do what we said we would do with the money?

❖ Did we spend what we were supposed to spend, more or less?

❖ We said we would hire ten people – did we hire ten people, or did we hire twenty?

For operational plans, the typical measure is key performance indicators (KPIs). When looking at production, it might be output, quality, deadlines or delays. For marketing, it can be market share, brand, brand recognition, customer satisfaction. In R&D, it is typically the number of new products, number of patents, etc. These KPIs are a clear indication of whether you are on track or not in achieving the operational targets you set.

But for the strategy, and the underlying vision, there are typically NO indicators! Often we simply rely on the operational plan's key performance indicators to measure whether a strategy was successful or not. But if you want to be thorough and disciplined then each type of plan must have its own indicators, otherwise you run the risk of attributing the wrong set of reasons to the lack of achievement. This means that you need to develop a specific set of indicators for measuring the success of your strategy. Where direct indicators cannot be applied, use proxies. For example, if you say that your dream is to become the technology leader in personal communications by 2008, how will you know that you are making progress on this? There are no direct measures. But there are proxies: articles written on the company around technological issues, use of the product by the ten companies you respect most for their technological leadership, number of patents, number of new products launched this year, last year, number of imitations. Alone, they might not be enough, but taken together, the number of patents I register, the number of companies that buy my products, and the size of my R&D budget probably tells me that I am becoming a technological leader.

Thus, it is not that strategic indicators do not exist or that they are difficult to design – it is simply that, because they require the creation of a new set of indicators, companies ignore them. Instead, most companies use the 'balanced' scorecard, which is a mistake. What you really want is a scorecard that is as 'imbalanced' as possible so that it fits your vision – which hopefully is not the same vision as that of your neighbor! It is essential that you build indicators that are unique to your vision.

it is not that strategic indicators do not exist or that they are difficult to design – it is simply that companies ignore them

Meaningful metrics

As we discussed above, every piece in the vision is measurable. Even when the piece to be measured can not be measured using financial metrics. Back to our favorite vision 'Let's win the hearts of Europe by

1996'. You can measure it on several dimensions – one is on the 'We' – have 'we' become a team? You can, on a regular basis, see whether there is more teamwork than before. The next piece of the vision is 'Win'. 'Win' is positive. Just as 'lose' is negative. And 'win the hearts' can be measured with such things as image studies – for example, is the image of Euro Disney Paris more positive than it was one or two or three years ago? Then there is 'Europe' – how has that evolved? Do we have a greater mix of customers from across Europe? How many of these articles are in popular magazine, compared to economic journals or French magazines? What is the spontaneous and knowledgeable awareness of Disney, in Europe compared to in France? And how has it evolved over time? Finally '1996': did we make the deadline? If not, why not, and how close are we?

In most cases you must define the metrics before you start implementing the vision. If you decide that it is important for all of your employees to receive ten days of training in the coming 12 months, then you need a way of measuring whether that training has happened, and you need to decide on what those metrics will be before you take action.

Rewarding what matters

Part of designing an organization that supports your vision is about designing measures that will encourage everyone to work in the desired direction. Incentives are one way of rewarding employees for working in the new direction. This goes back to the need for alignment and focus that we discussed in earlier chapters.

incentives are one way of rewarding employees for working in the new direction

Booz Allen Hamilton is an example of a company that changed its structure to fit its dream.[7] In the mid-1990s they launched Vision 2000 with the objective of moving from a company that worked regionally to one that would serve the needs of clients across the world, a change requested by many of their clients. To align the company with the vision, senior management completely changed the corporate structure:

- they combined regional practices into nine global practices;
- profit and loss was moved from the regions to the nine practices;
- two of the nine practices were region-specific, five were industry-based and the last two were functional.

Consequently, they also changed the incentive program of the partners to focus on the success of the entire firm, thereby encouraging cooperative behavior. Whereas before, every partner would receive a bonus solely based on the amount of *new* business he would bring, the new system took into account several new criteria that fostered cooperation. In the new system, the number of points awarded the partners depended on:

- mentoring
- market development
- quality of work
- billability
- adherence to partner's values.

In addition, performance appraisal was not based on a single manager but on the feedback from a team of 8–12 people. Forty-five per cent of the annual salary was in bonus form. This goes back to our arguments at the beginning of this chapter about the importance of creating structures, roles, responsibilities principles and processes that support the execution of your vision.

The devil is in the behavior

Over time, structures have a tendency to suffer from sclerosis, becoming detrimental rather than supportive of how the organization functions. Even in a flat hierarchical structure, silos appear. Some managers may be possessive of their teams and knowledge; or departments are used to working together and not with other parts of the business. Knowledge and best practices are not shared, the wheel is constantly being reinvented. These behaviours hamper the execution of the vision.

Fortunately, there are a number of things which you can do to stop that from happening.

Make sure that at the executive committee level you have members who are willing to ask for input from other members on the areas which they themselves have not mastered. This will force them to look beyond their area of expertise and forces everyone to be both citizens of their departments and corporate citizens. How many times do we see purely bilateral discussions between the CEO and each member of the executive committee during the meetings? And is this because the CEO has not developed the behaviour of encouraging all the members to question the issues raised by the other members – instead they remain silent, choosing not to provide their own viewpoint for fear of interfering, of trespassing on someone else's turf. Clearly, this type of behavior does not contribute to alignment and congruence in the achievement of the vision.

A second approach is to encourage employees to exchange seats. This is typically done through job rotations, or by asking people to take another person's place for a day or a week. Not only does this increase awareness of the different ways in which the organization can work together, but it also helps reduce conflict.

Finally, change the organizational structure often. Even the best structure will not last more than three to five years. Changing the structure will force people to embrace a different perspective. As another famous saying goes: change latitudes to change attitudes.

changing the structure will force people to embrace a different perspective

These are just some of the ways which can be used to avoid organizational atrophy by encouraging people to see things from someone else's perspective.

The power of no

Each time a new hierarchical level is created or a person is appointed to a management position, the chances are that he or she will prevent things from happening rather than encourage things to happen. This is what we term scenting (marking one's territory) and not leading. Those who have a dog and have moved houses with their pet, will understand exactly what we mean: the minute a dog arrives on his new territory, he sniffs every corner and urinates everywhere to mark his territory. And the bigger and more complex the territory, the more spots the dog marks.

The same goes for newly appointed managers, except that the marking of the territory is translated into stupid or constraining decisions that they make to prevent others from making their own decisions and taking action (or worse, a mix of both!)

Let us look at a recent example, as described by Jacques:

> I appointed a new director of operations for my company, Châteauform, in charge of all sites situated outside France. One of these sites is situated in a ski resort in the Swiss Alps. Teams of executives go there to work and ski or walk in the mountains. One of the first decisions of my newly appointed director was to cancel the international ski passes that allowed our staff to ski both on the French and Swiss sides of the Portes du Soleil, allowing only for seasonal ski passes for the Swiss side of the mountain.

This is about marking one's territory. Why? Because the decision completely contradicts the company's vision of being the most convivial, customer-oriented provider of training grounds. Part of this vision is about accompanying or meeting participants on the slopes to say hello, with wine or liquor, and guiding them in their trip. And a 'stupid' little cost-saving measure such as that one is perceived by the line people as a sign that things are changing inside the company. This could lead to a snowball effect of other 'small and stupid' decisions that smother the vision. Suddenly, we no longer see ourselves as close to the customer and making life easier for them, and the vision loses all meaning.

This attitude of nay-saying or constraining decisions and choices to reinforce who is boss and what lies within his or her territory is not uncommon. Most companies that choose to stay focused also stay flat (Google, Virgin and Nike) – they know that each additional hierarchical level will add another set of constraints and 'no's'.

Inevitably, the main problem lies in uncovering this type of territorial behavior so that it can be stopped, or better still, preventing it from happening in the first place.

> **most companies that choose to stay focused also stay flat – each additional hierarchical level will add another set of constraints**

First, knowing requires an open-door policy. This means that any employee can go to the level above to voice frustrations and doubts. It also calls for a certain degree of 'management by walking around'. Jacques learnt about the new rule when he asked the host of the site (all sites are managed by couples that host the participants) to meet his clients after a meeting was over and she replied, 'I can't, they are on the French side and my ski pass is for the Swiss side only.'

So, to prevent the piling up of 'no's', you need mechanisms for listening to the front line. Châteauform instituted a bi-monthly afternoon tea. Everyone is invited and anyone who wants to, can sit down to coffee, jam, jelly, pancakes and cakes and ask questions. For many years, at Virgin Atlantic Airways, any employees could openly talk to the CEO, Richard Branson. Access to the CEO can counter the slow build up of 'no's' by making the CEO aware of them.

Prevention is obviously even better than fixing what has gone wrong and is strongly linked to the selection criteria applied to new managers: do they fit with the company culture? Do they embrace the vision? Do they have a good track record of working in teams rather than creating pigeon-holes? When discussing their track record, do they say 'we' or 'I'? In this particular case, Jacques and his team did not listen carefully enough during the interviews that led to hiring the new operations director.

Just doing my job

How often are we, as consumers, met with blind, deaf, stubborn, blank faces and stares from the front-line person just 'doing their job', and feeling righteous about it? How much of a company's vision is

how much of the dream is waylaid in the brainless, robot-like interactions of a company's interface with its clients?

destroyed in this way? How much of the dream is waylaid in the brainless, robot-like interactions of a company's interface with its clients?

How can we find out about these destructive actions? Can they be avoided?

Managers and supervisors are hardly ever present when this type of incident happens – they are 'busy' managing. Even if you ask to see the boss, you will most probably be told that the person is unavailable at the moment – the interface is the one in charge of doing the brainless job! Will the incident be reported by the customer? Rarely! Customers are not brain surgeons – they have other things to do than revive flat encephalograms.

The best cure once again is prevention – it is the simplest and at the same time the most complex thing to do: focusing on the *why* before focusing on the *what* and *how* when explaining policies, procedures and the like to the front line so that they do not just do their job but can relate it to the why. This should be coupled with the second simplest most complex thing to do: empower employees to go beyond 'I am just doing my job'.

In companies we have a tendency to focus on policies, standards, and procedures, on the *what?* And *how?* Rather than on the *why?*

'In case of fire please do not take the elevator because fire propagates faster in chimney-like environments' would be a 'Why?' type of approach. But it is faster to simply say 'Don't take the elevator', 'Don't do this', 'Fill in this form', 'Cross this line'. But this approach doesn't encourage people to use their brains. This is blatantly obvious in the typical conversations between a boss and a subordinate:

Boss: what are you working on?

Subordinate: xyz ...

Boss: I'm not sure this should be your priority. Maybe you should focus on this (an alternative what) and do it this way (an alternative how).

Neither the boss nor the subordinate have considered the why – i.e. the perspective, the link to broader objectives, to the vision. The subordinate will be discouraged to take the initiative and will just 'do the job'. Yet empowerment is key to success. The key ingredients of a good empowering system include:

empowerment is key to success

- ❖ Define the scope of empowerment (full, limited to a certain area, amount, budget, or list of actions).
- ❖ Provide the means to take power: training, clarity of rules, (including escalation), culture of encouragement, information, perspectives, budgets.
- ❖ Select the people you empower. The broader the scope, the more 'rounded' people should be.
- ❖ Share which values and behaviors are encouraged and those which should be avoided.

Every dogma has its day

A vision is expressed, action plans are identified, and then ... nothing happens. It is often rules and regulations that get in the way of things happening.

it is often rules and regulations that get in the way of things happening

People have been told the why (vision), the what (action plans) and have started thinking about the how. They start inventing rules for every possible situation, ignoring the 80/20 principle (in 80 per cent of all cases, only 20 per cent of the rules and procedures are applicable and useful). This is often done with a lot of good will. Even worse, by thinking of extreme cases and how to solve them, they create rules that end up being adapted to mainstream problems, smothering the vision. This is illustrated by the well-known normal distribution curve shown in Figure 6.6.

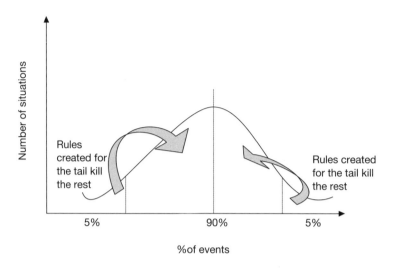

Figure 6.6 The Pareto principle reversed

This type of behaviour leads to the birth of the clandestine company. It is made up of a set of rules, regulations and procedures, which were absent from the original vision, and were created by those in charge of implementation, because they focused too much on trying to solve every situation. Instead of supporting the vision, they destroy it, whether out of good will or as a revolt against a vision with which they disagree. The entire implementation of the vision is affected. Let us give an example.

It is a well-known fact in the retailing world that between 0.5 and 6 per cent of cost of goods sold is merchandise stolen from the store. The reaction to this can be:

❖ Treat that 0.5–6 per cent as 'infrequent events' that can be minimized through better targeting, precautions, guards and anti-theft alarms on the goods and at the doors.

❖ Decide that it is a key part of the sales teams' responsibilities: don't let goods disappear from the store.

Nordstrom, a US department store, takes the first view. In fact, the first lines of the job description for sales associates say: 'You will meet any unreasonable demands from our customers'. In contrast, at the French department store Galeries Lafayette (at least at the time Jacques worked with them), the first line said: 'Your job is to protect the merchandise'.

The question is – if your vision is total customer satisfaction, which one of the two approaches is more likely to support your vision? At Nordstrom, a sales person will accompany a client to a different part of the store to help them with their purchase, while at Galeries Lafayette, rules and regulations mean that the sales person cannot leave their counter because they will be held responsible for any goods stolen in their area of responsibility.

How does one get rid of the clandestine corporation?

❖ First, never miss a chance to repeat the *why* and *what* of the business, so that the *how* is constantly put into perspective.

> **never miss a chance to repeat the *why* and *what* of the business, so that the *how* is constantly put into perspective**

❖ As we mentioned when we talked about reality checks, use your company as a normal client would, and not as a privileged executive. If not, you will not know what your customers experience. Try calling the general number (and not a direct line) to see how you are greeted ('press 1, 2, 3' 'all our lines are busy', etc.), buy your goods in the store and not the company warehouse; receive the same bill as your clients, etc.

❖ Have a 'kill the dogma' day once a year. Ask everyone, in teams, across all departments to put together a list of all the things that are preventing them from achieving the vision. You will find that most obstacles are the result of internal rules and regulations, created somewhere, at some point, by someone (or a team) but that no-one knows why or by whom, although they accept that they exist. Kill them immediately. It is normally very clear that those rules are clandestine: try asking who actually created them and no-one will know! Also, beware of rules created by well-meaning cross-functional teams – typically they have worked hard to ensure that no situation or person can escape their role model!

Spend as much time making things happen as time spent disentangling what is stopping things from happening. Getting rid of dysfunctions is your responsibility, and you must be willing to listen to your employees and deal with them. This goes back to our discussion on the devil is in the behavior.

Remember that dysfunctions stifle energy. When someone is repeatedly confronted with a hurdle or a bottleneck, they will give up unless they receive help that will allow them to keep going further. Some dysfunctions are explicit and easy to deal with (like replacing a machine), other are more delicate, like changing reporting lines. Take the example of the lost and found department of one of the major railway stations in France – the Gare de Lyon in Paris. When you call the department, they ask you to send a fax detailing your profile (name, phone number, etc.), what you lost, and when. Unfortunately for the vision of becoming a world-class service organization, the department has another rule: employees cannot make international phone calls. So they receive your fax from abroad but cannot call you back. The devil is indeed in the detail. ... The smart manager who decided that employees could not be trusted not to make private calls was the same one who stressed trust as an important component of the new service-oriented vision.

Summary

An organization needs to have a structure adapted to its vision. The two must be aligned. A number of structural mechanisms can support the implementation of the vision:

❖ Appoint champions who will ensure that corporate initiatives happen. One way of doing this is to appoint a champion for each of the key action points of your vision. Make sure these champions are close to the top, reporting directly to the CEO and that they are seasoned enough to be seen as legitimate.

❖ Redefine roles and responsibilities to match your targets. Whom you appoint for what sends strong signals about what you consider as important.

❖ Adapt the degree of coordination across your structure to your vision. This is closely linked to corporate advantage and to how headquarters will add value.

❖ Prefer principles over structure. They guide action better than structures do and resist better to shifts in strategy. They will help you build an organization that is focused on making things happen.

❖ Measure what matters. Set clear control mechanisms for your strategic plans, operational plans and budgets. Control allows us to assess whether the plan is on track or not, and if not, what needs to be done to get back on track.

❖ Reward what matters. Design rewards and incentives that will encourage everyone to work in the desired direction.

❖ Keep your structure healthy – get rid of the little, everyday actions that kill visions. These are found in everyday behavior that must be weeded out at the root: divisions, imposing decisions to demonstrate power, just 'doing my job' rather than understand the why, and the creation of a parallel, clandestine organization.

principles will help you build an organization that is focused on making things happen

NOTES TO CHAPTER 6

1 www.axa.com.

2 Christopher Bartlett, McKinsey & Company (1996). Managing knowledge and learning. Harvard Business School, case study 9-396-357.

3 Pinault-Printemps-Redoute (2000). Corporate management of a rapidly expanding international group. IMD case study. IMD-3-0868.

4 McKinsey & Company (1996). Managing knowledge and learning.

5 Lou Gerstner (2002). *Who Says Elephants Can't Dance*. HarperCollins, 23.

6 Grand Vision (1997). Management Principle Manual.

7 Gary Loveman and Jamie O'Connell (1996). Booz Allen & Hamilton: Vision 2000. Harvard Business School, case study 9-396-031.

7 Dreaming on ... with open eyes

Leadership is the art of accomplishing more than the science of management says is possible. COLIN POWELL

In this chapter we look at the cornerstones that support everything we have said so far. Together, discipline, trust, support and stretch not only help you execute your vision, they create an organization that is flexible and can adapt constantly to its environment.

discipline, trust, support and stretch not only help you execute your vision, they create an organization that is flexible

We will start by looking at Best Buy, whose carefully planned transformations, carried over as it adapted its vision, are a great example of flexibility and adaptability, and argue well for discipline, trust, support and stretch. We then move on to look at each of the four dimensions more specifically, and how balanced your organization is in terms of support, stretch, trust and discipline.[1] Finally, we look at how the four elements work together as mutually reinforcing aspects of execution and how to ensure that you have built a team that will foster stretch, support, trust and discipline.

With sales of US$27 billion in 2005, Best Buy was the largest consumer electronics retailer in North America. It had a compounded annual growth rate of 16 per cent when the industry average was 4.9 per cent. In May 2003, the company announced a new vision, based on customer centricity. The new concept was tested in 32 stores, and when results proved positive, Best Buy decided to roll them out to all of their 832 stores between 2005 and 2007.[2]

The company chose to go through a major transformation effort at a time when it was both successful and prosperous. But this type of approach was not new to the company – in fact, it had a history of transformation throughout its existence, which it crystallized as successive concepts over time.

Concept 1 focused on inventory turnover rather than unit margins and was all about making discount shopping fun. It came into being after the company's largest store was hit by a tornado. Family members and employees sold the remaining products at a discount on the company's parking lot. It was a huge success. Best Buy Concept 1 superstore opened in 1983. Five years later the chain was running 100 stores.

Forced into a price war against a major regional rival, Best Buy faced bankruptcy. In reaction, it launched *Concept 2*, which was an everyday, low-priced consumer electronics warehouse. As a result of the transformation, the company survived and reached a turnover of US$5 billion by 1994, but with very little margin.

Richard Schulze, CEO of Best Buy, decided to transform the company yet again. *Concept 3* (1995–98) and *Concept 4* (1998–2000) focused on helping consumers keep up to speed with technological innovations in consumer electronics and computers by providing some sales advice and helping grow margins.

Concept 5, introduced in 2001, focused on services and solutions, bringing together different types of products. By 2003, the company ran 679 stores and Best Buy had become the leader in its industry. Schulze retired to become chairman, appointing Brad Anderson as his successor.

Anderson decided it was time to transform the company yet again and created *Concept 7*. He believed that market size would not allow for Best Buy to run more than 1,000 stores profitably. Competition was intensifying, not only from Circuit City (half Best Buy's size in terms of revenue) but also from mass-market retails such as Wal-Mart and electronic retailers like Dell, Amazon.com and eBay. The digital revolution had brought together electronics, computers, data and video, with the result that pure consumer electronics companies only owned a third of the market.

Concept 6 was intentionally skipped to signal to the organization the importance of the change needed and the need to go beyond what had been done previously (*stretch*).

Customer centricity was at the heart of *Concept 7*. Anderson was sure that the company would succeed where other retailers had failed. The tradition was to focus on products and not on consumers. But Best Buy had a tradition of proving conventional wisdom wrong.

To start with, Best Buy had to quantify the profitability of their different customer segments, understanding why some were more interesting than others. Using this analysis, they came up with five potentially profitable segments for the company, defined in terms of consumer needs and behaviors (the family man, the focused, active younger male, the affluent professional, the suburban soccer mom, the small business customer) on which the company would focus to the exclusion of all others. The marketing team came up with a value proposition for each segment, translated into store layout, product assortment and tailored service, so that each store could cater in a different way to the needs of each segment. A total of 32 stores were selected as 'lab stores' to test the new concept. They were empowered to test the layout, assortment, try local marketing solutions, work on economies of scale and were encouraged to experiment (*Trust*). The increase in sales in these stores was between 12 per cent and 25 per cent.

The customer centricity initiative was supported by three other initiatives that dealt with controlling costs and investment spending, offering services with products (a specialist to help you set up your home cinema) and building partnerships with entertainment distributors such as Napster or Rhapsody (*Discipline* of focus). Costs and investments were controlled so as to allow complete focus on the new initiative (*Support*).

Customer centricity called for a change in culture, with a shift in power from headquarters to retail stores. What made the initiative a success was the trust, support, discipline and stretch that were present throughout the transformation.

The four cornerstones of continuous execution

The Best Buy example is a great story of a company that changes ahead of its time – i.e. it is proactive rather than reactive. Underpinning their execution are the four most important dimensions of execution: discipline, trust, support and stretch. These are the four cornerstones upon which the House Model is built.

1 **Discipline**. In this context everyone is disciplined to make things happen. When we say we will do something, we do it. We don't deviate. This is not discipline in the military sense of following an order, this is discipline in the sense of sticking to one's set priorities, focusing on what we have decided to do and choosing not to do other things.

2 **Trust**. Trust in your team and in the people you have with you. Trust leads to autonomy. It's about trust for people to experiment, to try, to make mistakes, to use their intuition.

3 **Support**. Money, energy, time, staff. There is no point in having a grand vision and then have no resources to put behind it. Resources need to be funneled into a single direction, which also means restraints in other ones.

> **there is no point in having a grand vision and then have no resources to put behind it**

4 **Stretch**. Accelerating rather than braking to think differently, going beyond the obvious. This gives 'taking people out of their comfort zone' its real meaning. It means breaking the rules of the game, of conventional wisdom to find new and unknown ways of being ahead.

Let us consider each dimension in greater detail.

Discipline

Discipline involves making sure that all the initiatives you launch are heading in the same direction. Otherwise you create the organizational fatigue we discussed previously. The basics of disciplined initiatives are the following:

❖ Focus – don't disperse your energy trying to be a jack of all trades.

❖ One umbrella, or big initiative, or concept launched at a time.

❖ Building blocks. What you want is a few initiatives, pushed forward for a long time (unless there is a need to break from your past), with each initiative building on the previous one. Remember what you did previously when you launch the new initiative or program. There must be a continuation from the previous initiative. For instance, in the case of Best Buy, Concept 7 was made possible because in Concepts 4 and 5 the company had already moved in the direction of selling services and not just products (such as total solutions) and trained their people to make technological complexity easier to understand.

❖ Make sure that all the initiatives have the same focus. For example, as we saw in Chapter 6, Welch at GE launched only ten major initiatives over the course of 20 years. And initiatives such as Six Sigma worked well because it came after Work Out, which had instilled a culture of open discussion and initiative taking.

It is therefore also important that you resist changing top management every few years. Each newly appointed senior executive wants to launch his or her own initiative. As a result, focus and discipline of execution are lost to the new 'flavor of the month'.

So, how are you doing with corporate discipline in your company?

❖ Do you focus? Do you choose to do things that you don't really want to do?

❖ Do you build successfully on what was previously done? Or do you build walls over time between different initiatives and programs?

❖ Are you prepared to let go of some of the things that you are doing or do you keeping adding and adding to the list?

❖ Can you name current initiatives that should be stopped and that have little impact on accomplishing your current vision?

❖ Can you stop them, or do they have a life of their own?

Trust

Trust is truly important in execution. Otherwise you are constantly looking over your shoulder, asking for explanations, justifications. The lack of trust has two negative implications:

❖ It slows down execution.

❖ You miss the opportunity of having several hierarchical levels that could help you execute the vision, simply because you feel as though everything needs to go through you.

There is a direct link between trust and the behaviors that you want to promote to accomplish the vision. If the company values are shared and espoused by your employees, their actions will fall within the realm of those values. You can therefore trust them to act in a way that supports your vision. Figure 7.1 shows the impact of values and trust on the amount of execution power.

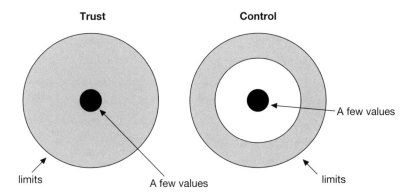

Figure 7.1 The difference between trust and support in terms of execution power

The shaded area represents the amount of autonomy available when we share a few values and limits. When there is trust, you can let people run with their ideas.

When you exercise control, there is a large area that includes everything that is not allowed, either because it does not correspond to the values (circle one) or because it is not delegated (circle two). Clearly, your ability to execute is diminished.

trust has an implication for the people you want to work with and the support given

Trust does have an implication for the people you want to work with and the support given. They need to:

- ❖ share the values
- ❖ have the required skills
- ❖ want autonomy.

These three points are preconditions to autonomy. In return you must provide your team with all the support, information and resources that they need to do their job well. And as a leader, you must be willing to delegate. Howard Schultz, the CEO of Starbucks, mentions in his book how one of the things he is most proud of is the culture of trust and support he has created in the organization.[3] And he stresses that this is not just words, but is about concrete actions such as a comprehensive healthcare program that is accessible even to part-timers and stock options that provide ownership for employees at all levels.

There are some instances where trust is quasi-obligatory – when you need speed. And you need speed when you are in trouble, in a crisis. Under those conditions there is no time to coach or control others. We should probably always function as though we were in a crisis situation. It is said that in crisis or turnaround situations, it can be very effective to apply the 1 : 10 : 100 rule, which is one leader, a team of ten trusted employees who report to the leader and who each have ten employees who report to them.

there is synergy between trust and discipline: it creates speed

There is synergy between trust and discipline: it creates speed. With focus, we don't go around chasing too many ideas and initiatives all at the same time, and we trust that everyone does so and is going in the same direction. It goes faster!

Is trust a must in your company?

❖ Do people share/espouse the values of your company?

❖ Are the limits explicit?

❖ Do people know about those limits? About the things that 'no-one does around here'?

❖ Are they equipped, in terms of skills, to be autonomous?

❖ Are individual, team initiatives reinforced through constant support or constant constraints?

❖ What score did your company get on trust in your last employee survey? Is it good?

Support

Support is about putting your money where your mouth is. GE spent US$2.5 billion on their Six Sigma initiative, training over 5,000 people to become black belts. In the end, the cost savings added up to US$5 billion, but it still takes guts to invest the original amount. That is support. Along with the financial support, Welch also appointed a Six Sigma champion who reported directly to the CEO. This type of appointment is important because:

❖ it signals the importance of the initiative

❖ it becomes a corporate priority

❖ you don't need to spend a lot of time working on convincing others – you just needed to say that you have been sent by the CEO.

In the case of Best Buy, the 32 pilot stores represented an investment of US$20 million, a little over 20 per cent of profit. A pilot store was started close to the company headquarters so that the CEO and his team could go and observe the experiment often. In this way, the senior team demonstrated the importance of the initiative as well as their support.

So support requires both investment in different types of resources (money, time, people) and a champion (as described in Chapter 6).

Together with disciplined focus, support allows you to demultiply – spending US$100 on ten projects does not have the same impact as spending US$100 on a single project! It really is a killer combination! And the impact is bigger! The learning of what works or not is faster!

Often we lose faith in initiatives, even end them, because we think that they are not working. And we think that they are not working because we have not given them our maximum effort, and the reason we did not was either because we were scared and skeptical right from the start or because we were spread too thinly across too many initiatives. But we should think the other way round – for any pilot, test or initiative launched, if it does not work under maximum effort conditions it will never work under normal conditions!

Where do you stand with initiatives and support in your organization?

❖ What initiatives are currently underway?

❖ How many in total?

❖ Do they all contribute to making your vision happen?

❖ Are they all well funded? Provided with appropriate resources?

❖ Are they well prioritized?

❖ Given the current state, can you say that you can give each one maximum effort?

❖ If the answer is no, what would you cut? What would you reinforce?

❖ Are all of your champions at the right level with the right agenda?

Stre-e-e-t-c-h

Stretch is about pushing people beyond their comfort zone, giving them stretch goals and objectives. Stretch goals lead to better execution – being forced to go beyond what you can do will force you to find new ways. There are several ways in which you can stretch your organization:

❖ Encouraging bottom–up initiatives. Every time you ask 'Is there any other way?' or 'What is your second best solution?' or 'What do you suggest we should do?' you are stretching people because they have to think beyond the current behavior or stimulus response.

❖ New situations. Job rotation, expatriation or asking employees to put themselves in someone else's shoes, be it from a different department or a customer, is a good way of providing new insight and stimuli. In the new situation, you can then ask them to implement what they proposed.

❖ Exposure is a similar way of stretching people. Exposing employees to things which they are not used to. This could be benchmarking with other companies in a radically different industry, or taking them on a trip to an exotic, different location to force them to reflect on similarities, differences and come up with creative scenarios and options.

When Euro Disney redesigned its vision, they agreed that is was hard for the team to win the hearts of Europe with most of them being either French or American. As a result, they decided to run their executive committee meetings in different countries in Europe. The meetings lasted two full days each time. So, for example, when the meeting was held in Holland, guest speakers came to talk about the impact of religion on business values, the more feminine dimensions of the Dutch culture, and their straightforward way of communicating.

The executive committee walked around the streets, sampled foods and visited stores. The following meetings were held in Barcelona, in Munich, in Milan and in London. This gave the executive team unique insight into the way different European countries would react to the offering of Euro Disney, and how Disney needed to adapt to Europe.

Stretch is also about having the courage to employ people who know nothing about your business, or your industry. Take for example the bank First Direct, at the time of its launch. Half of their staff were people who had no previous knowledge of banking. They were what we call 'unconsciously incompetent' – they did not know what was not possible, which means that they generated more innovation and more

stretch and trust generate self-confidence

energy than the consciously incompetent! Yet the bank made *The Times'* list of the 100 best companies to work for in 2006.

Stretch and trust generate self-confidence. Self-confidence helps people dare. With daring, it is not necessary to have detailed plans about everything; instead you provide a sense of direction with people doing what it takes to go in that direction. This is where a vision takes its full meaning. The destination is given, everyone contributes to making the boat sail in that direction and take whatever initiatives it requires to adapt to the wind, the sea and unforeseen circumstances.

Linking the four

There is a direct link between the four factors – discipline, trust, support and stretch – that contribute to execution, as depicted in Figure 7.2.

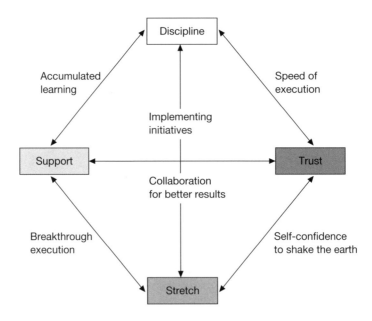

Figure 7.2 The four elements of continuous execution

If my boss trusts me when taking me out of my comfort zone, I will come up with new ideas. He trusts me to make these ideas happen. My self-confidence increases, and as it increases, I willingly leave my comfort zone and try other new ideas. (*Trust* and *stretch* leading to increased *self-confidence*.) And as I receive significant support doing it, I go beyond conventional wisdom. Together, *stretch* and *support* lead to *breakthrough execution*, because not only do you get execution, but you get execution with new ways (which in turn increases the differentiation of the company). Together *trust* and *support* lead to greater *collaboration* and *team work*, for the better sharing of ideas and best practices. *Discipline* and *support* create a *knowledge culture*, while *discipline* and *trust* lead to speed, because there is no checking and double-checking of every initiative and experiment launched. It also means that you will not have to be as involved in the details, freeing up your time. As for *discipline* and *stretch*, they lead to *innovative execution*. This is about constant transformation, with initiatives being increasingly innovative over time.

Are you ready for transformation to achieve your vision?

Look at the four elements in Figure 7.2 and ask yourself:

❖ Which of the four elements is well developed in our company?

❖ Which of the four elements is underdeveloped in our company?

❖ What are we able to achieve where and when the links exist (i.e. when two of the elements are well developed)?

❖ What are we unable to achieve when two elements do not have the same level of development, and the linkages are weak?

❖ What actions do we need to take to improve?

Built to be different

Stretch, trust, support and discipline are strongly related to the qualities of the people who are in charge of executing the vision. This means that selecting your team becomes a critical task. There are two things to bear in mind when selecting your team:

❖ **Complementarity** (different profiles). Your team members must complement each other. For example, if among your team members there is a person with a dominant action orientation and you are thinking about making an acquisition, the person with the action bias might make a too quick buy/don't buy decision, while the person that has a planner orientation will be more analytical but maybe too slow. By having complementarity you make better decisions as the top team. There are a number of tools available to help you assess this degree of complementarity.

❖ **Internal promotion**. For effective implementation you need people who come from within the organization. Seventy per cent of the management team should come from inside, thirty per cent from outside. Why? Because they know the organization, they have a network, which means that it will be easier for them to get help from other departments. This in turn will result in greater cooperation and speed of action. However, you may not be aware that there are other ways of dealing with the problem and you might try to reinvent the wheel. This is why you need part of your team to be from the outside.

In turnaround situations, it is likely that the team chosen for making it happen comes from within, after having fired those who created the mess. As the CEO of adidas said when he took over the helm of the company:

> It is true that I needed to let go of the top people, but by promoting those just below, rather than hiring from the outside, I unleashed a great deal of energy. I trusted them to help me deliver on my vision of becoming the best sports brand in the world. They knew the business, had ideas which had been blocked by their bosses, and were ready to move with speed.[4]

If you decide, however, to hire senior executives from the outside, and in particular from a company bigger than yours, to support the implementation of your vision, starve them!

As a retail group began to expand internationally, it decided to hire a new CIO from the outside, from a company five times its own size (100,000 as opposed to 20,000 employees), rather than promote one of the retailer's IT directors. What a mistake! Two years down the line, the IT budget had gone from 2 per cent of sales to 4 per cent. A centralized team of 75 people had been created to give birth to a monster new IT platform which would supposedly do everything. Three years later, the executive, the team and the new platform were dumped. Applying to a small company in a different stage of development what had worked in a mega-retail group was not the solution. Had the executive been starved for resources, he would have been forced to think differently and come up with a creative solution to the company's IT challenges.

Finally, remember that if you have a common vision, and if everyone agrees on the why, you don't need to be specific with the strategy. But for this to happen, all of the members you select must have bought into the vision.

Tips for hiring senior executives

Ask the person you want to recruit to sit in a car beside you while you drive. Ask them to give you directions to get somewhere using a map. This will demonstrate their ability to plan, to control, to communicate, to coach, to foresee questions and answer them. Try it, it is a fantastic test!

Is your team complementary or too similar?

❖ Describe in one word what each member of your executive team is best at (for example, action-oriented, analytical, deliberative, positive).

❖ Is there complementarity or do you have too many people of the same type?

If the profiles and preferences are too close, whom should you hire given your current vision? Who is not indispensable to its achievement?

If there is a nice fit, a nice complementarity, how can you use each member's skills best while giving them responsibility for a major initiative that will be key in the execution of the vision (champion)?

Conversely, which projects should not be allocated to specific team members because of the gap in their profile/preferences and the initiative?

Summary

Discipline, trust, support and stretch are essential to building a flexible and adaptive organization that can continuously transform itself to achieve the vision.

Discipline

Discipline is primarily about making sure that you consistently sail the set course – that you remain focused, that you choose a select number of initiatives that build on each other, and that they go in the same direction. Discipline is also about continuity and trying to create a team of senior managers that can take the initiatives full circle, avoiding the flavor of the month, territorial-marking syndrome discussed in Chapter 6.

Trust

Trust is important for several reasons:

❖ It avoids you having to look over your shoulder all the time, slowing down execution and losing the benefits of trusting others to help you execute.

❖ There is a direct link between the behaviors that are important to the execution of the vision and trust. If the behaviors are part of the company fabric, then the decisions taken by your employees will automatically support the vision.

❖ Trust means having people who share the values, have the required skills and want autonomy. In return, you must provide the degree of support, information and resources required to do the job well. Trust also means that you must be willing to delegate.

trust means having people who share the values, have the required skills and want autonomy

Support

Support is about putting your money where your mouth is. Support requires both investment in terms of resources (money, time, people) and in appointing people who will execute the initiatives that will support the implementation of the vision (champions). Support means giving each chosen initiative maximum effort.

Stretch

Stretch is about taking people outside of their comfort zone, encouraging them to come up with innovative, creative ways that will lead to better execution. You can stretch your organization by:

❖ encouraging bottom–up initiatives

❖ putting employees into new situations, including job rotation, expatriation or by putting them in the place of the customer.

❖ encouraging exposure, which can be anything from external benchmarking to traveling to different and exotic locations.

Stretch is also about having the courage to employ people who know nothing about your business, or your industry, so that they can introduce new ideas.

Discipline, trust, support and stretch mutually enhance and reinforce each other, leading to great execution. *Trust* and *stretch* lead to increased *self-confidence*, they encourage employees to dare. *Stretch* and *support* lead to *breakthrough execution*, increasing the differentiation of the company. *Trust* and *support* lead to greater *collaboration* and *team work*. *Discipline* and *support* create a *knowledge culture*, while *discipline* and *trust* lead to greater speed – everyone is going together in the same direction. As for *discipline* and *stretch*, they lead to *innovative execution*, which is continuous transformation at its best.

Naturally, these four elements are dependent on the quality of your top team. Make sure that you select team members who are complementary, helping you make balanced decisions. Also, whenever possible, promote from within. The people who are already part of the organization know of your business, and have a network, which means you will gain in terms of greater cooperation and speed of action. However, you do need a portion of your team (something like 30 per cent) to be outsiders, bringing in new ideas and little luggage.

NOTES TO CHAPTER 7

1   For earlier work on these, please refer to
   ● Sumantra Ghoshal and Christopher A. Bartlett (1994). Linking organizational context and managerial action: the dimensions of quality of management; *Strategic Management Journal*, vol. 15, 91–112.
   ● Bala Chakravarthy (1996). The process of transformation in search of Nirvana. *European Management Journal*, 529–539.
2   Balaji Chakravarthy and Henri Bourgeois (2005). BestBuy. Staying at the top. IMD case study IMD-3-1430.
3   Schultz Howard (1997). *Pour Your Heart Into It*. Hyperion.
4   Company information.

Conclusion: Just dream it!

*Effort and courage are not enough
without purpose and direction.* PRESIDENT JOHN F. KENNEDY

In this concluding chapter you will find two things. The first section, called 'Early warning questions', is a list of questions that will help you decide whether you are ready to create and implement a dream with a deadline and what your chances of succeeding are. Even as you prepare to dream it is important to be realistic.

In the second half of the chapter you will find a succinct overview of what we have looked at in this book. It is not a summary of the summaries but rather brings all the different elements both of the House Model and its implementation together.

Early warning questions

Are you ready to define your dream?

- ❖ Is your horizon long enough to allow people to dream?
- ❖ Do you feel that routine and sleepiness have taken over your company?
- ❖ Are divides preventing your company from coming up with breakthrough thinking?
- ❖ Do you see your best people leave?

❖ Do you find that no new ideas are emerging from your long-range strategic planning process?

❖ Do you feel that your people lack enthusiasm for your company?

❖ Do you have difficulties pushing for new ideas in your organization?

❖ Do you see those who report immediate to you 'protecting' you by hiding certain realities and uncertainties and only reporting what they think you would like to hear?

❖ Do you feel the social and psychological distance between you and your company increase?

❖ Do you receive a warm welcome and standing ovations when you make your annual speech or polite applause with no or miscellaneous questions?

❖ When you invite your people to the annual dinner and you sit down at a table first, do a lot of people come and join you spontaneously?

❖ Do you hear a buzz and feel a high energy level everywhere in the company?

❖ Do you feel sufficiently comfortable with the financial analysts to share with them your story about the future or would you prefer to stick to the last quarter?

❖ Are all current initiatives reinforcing each other and going in the same direction?

❖ Does everyone in your organization know where the company is going?

Will you succeed?

❖ Have you involved enough people to express the vision?

❖ Did the vision become a 'natural' output or did it take a lot of forcing?

❖ Did you share it with the board? Was their reaction positive?

❖ Did you share it with the janitor? Did they like it?

❖ Did you share it with all your employees?

❖ Did you get rid of all those who were opposed to the vision?

❖ Is it simple enough to be understood by everyone?

❖ Is it measurable and measured?

❖ Does it have the key elements that will help you gain sustainable competitive advantage?

❖ Are all plans, individual objectives and annual resource allocations congruent with it?

❖ Have you selected the *few* top–down corporate initiatives that will help make it happen?

❖ Do you revisit it with a critical eye as to the underlying assumptions?

❖ As you reach the deadline, have you created the buzz that goes with reaching the goal?

❖ Is behavior disciplined? If not, what prevents discipline from happening?

❖ Are most people compliant or committed?

❖ Do you sincerely believe in the dream? Or is it just a gimmick? If so, just forget it. It was nice of you to read up to this point!

In a nutshell

The environment in which companies operate will not become less challenging. On the contrary, it will become increasingly complex, interconnected, unpredictable and competitive. The last thing a company wants in this type of environment is a muddled and complicated strategy formulation process that comes up with a bland, tasteless picture of the future.

Most senior executives actually recognize that the process of strategic planning is no longer useful – fraught with politics and power games.

It is too time-consuming and lengthy to develop, too incremental, too far from the field, too analytical and too compliant. To achieve sustainable success in this environment, companies need to design visions that are inspiring, that generate commitment and energy. A vision must be more than a beautifully crafted statement, an advertising slogan. It must be a dream with a deadline.

A vision must be more than a beautifully crafted statement, an advertising slogan; it must be a dream with a deadline

This dream must be short and inspiring, yet achievable. It should reflect the degree of urgency of the current situation, in a way that is credible. And it must carry a deadline, allowing progress and success to be measured and rewarded. Above all, we advocate a vision that is shared by all parties in the organization, calling for commitment rather than compliance. In this book, we have gone so far as to say that it may even be better to have a vision that is shared rather than a vision that is right.

The House Model is both at the heart of, and the first step in, the journey, a tool that will help you deliver a vision that is inspirational, a story that will generate commitment. It is a powerful way of keeping the process simple. Expressing a vision on a single page forces choices and prioritization. It encourages an honest appraisal about what really is achievable and what is desirable. Together, the roof (where you want to go), the pillars (how you will get there) and the foundation (the behaviors) tell the story of your dream.

The model leaves no option for delegation, scapegoating. Those people who are responsible for its execution are also responsible for its design. The architect is also the mason. Encouraging participation makes the vision much easier to implement than a top–down dictate. Of course, we acknowledge that it is not an easy exercise – working on a single page, making decisions that are all about implementing the dream, call for selectiveness, consistency, focus, accountability. This requires the ability to project a future and work backwards to fill in the gap, in a very concrete manner. And as a set of steps towards the future, the vision needs to be reviewed every year, making sure that you are going in the right direction. In this respect, the letter of intent helps ground the dream by serving as a basis for budgets and targets.

The two-day workshop is a proven method for making the dream with a deadline take off. Putting all those involved with the execution of the vision into the same room, building a common dream generates commitment and energy. Sharing information, and then agreeing on a dream and how to cascade it across the organization are critical steps in implementing the vision. Naturally, designing this two-day workshop calls for preparation in terms of the inputs – how to think differently about the business (trends, new markets, customer surveys), and the environment (opportunities) assessing where the company is (flash surveys, reports) versus where it wants to go. The presence of the CEO is important in that only he or she can ask for the level of commitment that this model demands. Getting the board and the CEO to participate is the ideal situation.

Once agreed on, the dream needs to be shared both with the board (if they did not participate in the workshop) and across the organization. The team involved in cascading the vision need to decide who will share what with whom, what formats will be used and what processes need to be in place to get feedback. Remember that understanding why a company has chosen a specific path generates a feeling of ownership. Talk about the *why* and not only about the *how* and *when*. The entire process must be planned thoroughly, for maximum impact, consistency and focus.

This is where the issue of discipline comes in. The two-day workshop is the fun part of the process. After that, discipline is required to make the vision happen. Remember that discipline is the daily demonstration of focus around something you have decided to do. It breeds consistency. Fortunately, there are ways of working on discipline. In terms of personal (leadership) discipline, your focus is demonstrated through a variety of symbols and signals, for example the types of issues that you focus on, the language you use, how you interact and ask questions, who gets appointed and who is invited to meetings. Even what you celebrate is a symbol of what you consider important.

Then there is the matter of corporate discipline. This is about following though on initiatives, (and avoiding the 'flavor of the month' syndrome), and when needed, using an umbrella approach under which to group initiatives. It is also very much about staying closely in touch with your business on a daily basis. Finally, it is about acting on ideas, turning them into action, disseminating good ideas, and appointing champions to support implementation.

With time, exercising discipline becomes part of the organization's fabric. The success of a vision depends on an organizational design that supports the execution of that vision. However, while structures can be modified to support a vision, they are often seen as being too mechanistic and often result in confining people into roles or pigeon-holes. In some cases, it is preferable to work with principles and processes rather than try to change existing structures. If principles are recognized and shared by all employees, they support action better than structures do. They are also more malleable, adapting to necessary changes in the strategy.

While discipline is about making sure that all the initiatives you launch go in the same direction and that you consistently walk your talk, three other behaviors are crucial in building an organization that is flexible and will be able to change its environment or adapt to it as need be.

Trust speeds up execution and allows you to rely on a great many more people to implement, because you do not feel as though you need to control everything. There is also a direct link between trust and the desired behaviors (what we call the foundations of the House Model). If everyone in the company shares the same values, their actions will fall within the realm of those values.

Support is about putting your money where your mouth is. It requires investing resources (people, time and money) into what has been recognized as important to the execution of the vision, and it means allocating strong leaders to champion the initiatives.

Finally, stretch is about encouraging people to go beyond their comfort zones, experiment and propose new ways of doing things, agreeing to, and then achieving, stretch goals.

Index

achievability 12
acquisitions 91
action 131
  action lists 76
  actions and milestones 12, 18, 22, 24–5, 31–2, 65–6
  sharing the vision and areas for 82–3
  turning ideas into action 113–14
adaptability 146–8
  see also continuous execution
adidas 32–5, 50, 97, 158
airlines, low-cost 56
allocation of resources 28, 39–41, 132–3
Amazon 1–2, 7
analysis, and intuition 7
Anderson, Brad 147, 148
annual review 38, 90–1, 166
appointments 139
  corporate symbols and signals 102–3
  selecting people from different backgrounds 111
  senior executives 158–9
Arla 5–6, 16
ARM Holdings 49
Armstrong, Neil 13
Asahi 56–8
astonishment report 101
AXA 118–19

baby boomers 52, 53
balanced scorecard 134
Bata 37
beer industry 56–8

behaviours
  identifying behavioral changes 83
  organizational dysfunction 136–44
  supporting behaviours 18, 22–3, 25, 63, 65–6
Beinhocker, Eric 4–5
Best Buy 109–10, 120, 146–8, 150, 153
Best Foods 55
Bezos, Jeff 1–2
Blank, Arthur 17
board 26
  sharing the vision with 76–81
Boeing 11
Booz Allen Hamilton 135–6
bottom-up initiatives 155
boundaries, redefining 49–51
Bourguignon, Philippe 79–80
Branson, Richard 139
breakthrough execution 156, 157
British Petroleum (BP) 111
'broad brush' approach xiv
Brown, John 111
budget plans (budgets) 40–1, 132–4
Bush, George (Senior) 3
business contexts 27
  multibusiness context 27–30
business model, reinventing 55–9
business performance, boosting 126
business unit level 27–30

cancellation policies (hotels) 112
cascading the vision 75, 81–5, 167
cashing out 54

celebrating 103–4
centralization 127–9
champions 107, 120–2, 125–6, 153–4
Châteauform 12, 40, 101, 104, 112, 138,
    139
chief executive officer (CEO) 81
  open-door policy 139
  role in two-day workshop 67–8, 167
Chrysler 105
clandestine organization 141–4
clanning 54
Club Med 79–80
collaboration 156, 157
commitment 7–8, 75, 85–9, 167
  letting go employees without 89–90
communication 84–5
  consistency of internal
      communication 85
Compagnie Générale des Eaux 41–3
comparative advantage 27
compensation 87
competitive advantage 27
complementarity 158
compliance 7–8, 75
Conran, Terence 20
consistency 25, 26, 29, 31, 85, 95
consumer research 61, 62
continuous execution 146–62, 168
  cornerstones 149–56
  discipline 149, 149–51, 156–7, 160,
      168
  linking the cornerstones 156–7
  selecting the team 157–60
  stretch 149, 154–6, 156–7, 161, 168
  support 149, 153–4, 156–7, 161, 168
  trust 149, 151–3, 156–7, 160–1, 168
control mechanisms 133
COOP 111
cooperation 124–6, 136
coordination 124–6
  mechanisms and centralization 128,
      129
corporate advantage 28–9, 126

corporate discipline 105–14, 167–8
  building initiatives on one another
      105–9, 150
  continuous execution 149, 149–51,
      156–7, 160, 168
  staying in touch 110–13
  turning ideas into action 113–14
  umbrella initiatives 109–10, 150
corporate headquarters
  coordination 124–6
  size 126–9
corporate level 27–30
corporate symbols and signals 97–105
  appointments 102–3
  celebrating 103–4
  deadlines 101
  interactions 99–100
  issues 97–8
  language 98–9
  meetings and team composition
      101
  physical settings 100–1
  questions 99
crises 152
cross-buying 99
cross-selling 99, 117
customer centricity 110, 118–20, 146,
      148
customer segments 118–20, 148
customers
  executives undergoing the normal
      customer experience 111, 143
  reality checks and 38
  trends 51–5, 61–2

Daimler 105
Danfoss 50
Daniel, Ron 123
deadlines 101
decisions, territorial behaviour and
      137–9
Dejouany, Guy 41–2
detailed strategic planning xiv

discipline 14, 94–115, 167–8
building initiatives on one another
105–9, 150
continuous execution 149, 149–51,
156–7, 160, 168
corporate discipline 105–14, 167–8
corporate symbols and signals
97–105
personal discipline 96–105, 167
staying in touch 110–13
turning ideas into action 113–14
umbrella initiatives 109–10, 150
distance, strategic planning and 7
divisions 129, 136–7
dogma 141–4
dream with a deadline (roof of House
Model) 17–18, 20–1, 23–4, 63, 65
Dreyfuss, Robert-Louis 97
dysfunctional behaviour 136–44
clandestine organization 141–4
divisions 136–7
imposing decisions to demonstrate
power 137–9
'just doing my job' 139–41

early warning questions 163–5
easyjet 56
Edison, Thomas A. 116
egonomics 54
80/20 principle 141
employees
dysfunctional behaviour 136–44
empowerment 139–41
internalization of the vision 85–8
letting go employees that do not buy
in to the vision 89–90
new situations 137, 155
perceptions 47, 59–60, 63, 64, 69–71
empowerment 139–41
enthusiasm 7–8, 85–9
Euro Disney 13, 64, 101, 111
Disney Style 122
reality checks 39

sharing the vision 84, 89–90
stretch 155
Everest tragedy 94–5
exposure 155
external appointments 158, 159
external perspectives *see* perspectives

fantasy adventure 54
Federal Express 129–30
financial holding 126–7
financial metrics 31, 134–5
financial objectives 40–1
First Direct 155–6
Fischer, Scott 94–5
flash survey 59–60, 69–71
flexibility 146–8
see also continuous execution
focus 31, 96, 150
focus groups 61, 62
followers, lack of 38
Ford Motor Company 3, 11
formula developer 126–7
formulation of the vision 14, 46–72
inputs 47
perceptions 47, 59–60, 63, 64,
69–71
perspectives 47, 48–59, 63, 64
proofs 47, 61–2, 62–3
two-day workshop 46–7, 62–8, 167
foundations (supporting behaviours)
18, 22–3, 25, 63, 65–6
Fourtou, Rene 43
front line, executives and 111

Galeries Lafayette 142–3
Gare de Lyon lost and found
department 144
General Electric (GE) 4, 83, 120, 127,
150, 153
champions 120–1, 153
corporate discipline 106–9
roles and responsibilities 122–3
Geox 1, 7

Gerstner, Lou 128–9
Giro 3
Giscard d'Estaing, Henri 80
Goethe, Johann Wolfgang von 46
golden oldies (baby boomers) 52, 53
Grand Optical 99–100
GrandVision 59, 100, 130–1

Hackman, Gene 57
Hall, Rob 94–5
Havas 43
headquarters *see* corporate
    headquarters
Hewlett Packard (HP) 3, 102–3
Higishi, Hirotaro 57
Hill, T. 9
Hindustan Lever 49
Honda 3
Horovitz, Jacques 12, 138, 139
hotel cancellation policies 112
House Model 13–14, 17–45, 166
    advantages 14
    application of 14
    business contexts 27
    challenges of the model 31–2
    comparison of one-page and
        three-page versions 36
    foundations 18, 22–3, 25, 63, 65–6
    fourth pillar 80, 81
    house rules 23–6
    letter of intent 39–41, 166
    multibusiness context 27–30
    participation in design 26–7, 166
    pillars 18, 21–2, 24–5, 63, 65–6
    reality checks 37–9
    roof 17–18, 20–1, 23–4, 63, 65
    three-page version 32–7
    two-day workshop to create 46–7,
        62–8, 167
HSBC 49

IBM 128–9
ideas, turning into action 113–14

IMD 50–1
incentives 128–9, 135–6
inclusiveness 31
India 49
indicators 133–4
individual discipline *see* personal
    discipline
individual objectives 40–1
industry boundaries 49–51
initiative fatigue 105–6
initiatives
    building on one another 105–9, 150
    umbrella approach 109–10, 150
innovative execution 157
inputs 47–62
    perceptions 47, 59–60, 63, 64,
        69–71
    perspectives 47, 48–59, 63, 64
    proofs 47, 61–2, 62–3
inspiration 11, 12
institutional discipline *see* corporate
    discipline
insurance industry 117–19
interactions
    corporate symbols and signals
        99–100
    Disney Style initiative 122
internal perceptions *see* perceptions
internal promotion 158–9
internalization of the vision 85–8
international operator 126–7
intuition, analysis and 7
issues 97–8

Japan 52
    beer industry 56–8
job rotation 137, 155
'just doing my job' 139–41

Kaplan, Sarah 4–5
Kennedy, John F., 'man on the moon'
    speech xii, 13, 19, 73
key performance indicators (KPIs) 133

key ways 18, 21–2, 24, 65–6
'kill the dogma' day 143
King, Martin Luther, 'I have a dream'
    speech 19, 20
Kirin 56–8
knowledge culture 156, 157
knowledge management 123

language 74, 81–2
    corporate signals and symbols
        98–9
leadership 14–15
    management and 8
    quality of 67
letter of intent 39–41, 166
low-cost airlines 56

'man on the moon' speech (Kennedy)
    xii, 13, 19, 73
management, and leadership 8
Marcus, Bernie 17
market research 61, 62
Maygold, Glynn 85
McKinsey & Company 123
measurement 12, 131–5
    measurability of actions and
        milestones 22, 31–2
    metrics 31, 134–5
    plans and 132–4
meetings 101
mega-trends 51–5, 61–2
Messier, Jean-Marie 41–3
metrics 31, 134–5
Microsoft 3, 11
Miles, Sandra 85
milestones, actions and 12, 18, 22,
    24–5, 31–2, 65–6
mission 2–3
    adidas 32–3
    SouthWest Airlines 86
mobile phones 50, 51
Mount Everest tragedy 94–5
multibusiness context 27–30

nay-saying 137–9
New Balance 52–3
new situations 137, 155
Nietzsche, Friedrich 94
Nike 3, 50
Nokia 6, 49
Nordstrom 142–3

objectives 40–1
observation 61–2
Ochiai, Nobuhiko 57, 58
1 : 10 : 100 rule 152
open-door policy 139
operational plans 132–4
organizational design 14, 116–45, 168
    champions 107, 120–2, 125–6, 153–4
    clandestine organization 141–4
    cooperation and coordination 124–6
    dysfunctional behaviours 136–44
    empowerment 139–41
    measurement of progress 131–5
    metrics 31, 134–5
    plans 132–4
    preventing organizational atrophy
        136–7
    principles and processes 129–31, 168
    rewards 103–4, 135–6
    roles and responsibilities 122–4
    size of corporate headquarters 126–9
    supporting the vision 116–20
    territorial marking 137–9
organizational fatigue 136–7
ownership 8

participation 26–7, 166
perceptions 47, 59–60, 63, 64, 69–71
Performance through People Award 85
personal discipline 96–7, 167
    corporate signs and symbols 97–105
perspectives 47, 48–59, 63, 64
    business model 55–9
    customer trends 51–5, 61–2
    industry boundaries 49–51

physical settings 100–1
pigeon-holes 129, 136–7
pillars 18, 21–2, 24–5, 63, 65–6
Pinault Printemps Redoute (PPR)
    124–6
plans 132–4
Polegato, Moretti 1
Popcorn, Faith 55
positive psychological contract 85
Powell, Colin 146
principles 129–31, 168
procedures 141–4
processes 129–31, 168
project teams 120
promotion, internal 158–9
proofs 47, 61–2, 62–3
proxies 31–2, 134
psychological contract 85

qualitative listening 61–2
quantitative data 61–2
questions
    corporate signals and symbols 99
    early warning questions 163–5
    reality checks and 38–9

readiness to define the vision 163–4
realism 12
reality checks 37–9
regulations 141–4
rejection of the vision 79
resources
    allocation of 28, 39–41, 132–3
    starving externally appointed senior
        executives 159
    support and continuous execution
        149, 153–4, 156–7, 161
responsibilities, roles and 122–4
review, annual 38, 90–1, 166
rewards 135–6
    corporate symbols and signals 103–4
risk 28
risk aversion 6–7

roles and responsibilities 122–4
roof of House Model 17–18, 20–1,
    23–4, 63, 65
rules 141–4

Sapporo 57, 58
scenario planning 48–9
scenting 137–9
Schultz, Howard 1, 9–10, 23, 88, 152
Schulze, Richard 147
Seagram 43
selection of team 157–60
selectivity 31
self-confidence 156, 157
seminars, cancellation policies and 112
shared vision 13
sharing the vision 14, 67, 73–93, 167
    board 76–81
    cascading 75, 81–5, 167
    dealing with employees who do not
        buy in 89–90
    internalization of the vision 85–8
    reviewing the vision 38, 90–1, 166
Shell 48
shoplifting 142–3
signals 96–7, 167
    corporate symbols and signals
        97–105
silver generation (baby boomers) 52, 53
simplicity 32
SKF bearings 50
Sony 11
SOS (save our society) 55
SouthWest Airlines 85–8
Soviet Union xv
speed 152, 156, 157
stability, illusion of 5–6
Starbucks 9, 23, 88–9, 152
staying in touch 110–13
strategic planning 4
    difference from visioning xvi, 10
    limitations xiii–xv, 4–8, 165–6
    SWOT analysis 9–10

strategic plans 132–4
stretch 149, 154–6, 156–7, 161, 168
success, chances of 164–5
Suntory 57
Super Dry Beer 57–8
support 149, 153–4, 156–7, 161, 168
supporting behaviours 18, 22–3, 25, 63,
    65–6
Swissair xiv
SWOT analysis 9–10
symbols 96–7, 167
   corporate symbols and signals
    97–105
synchronicity 26, 29–30
synergies 28, 126, 127–8

team composition 101
team selection 157–60
territorial marking 137–9
Tetra Pak 110
3M 2, 3
three-page House Model 32–7
trends, customer 51–5, 61–2
trust 149, 151–3, 156–7, 160–1, 168
two-day workshop *see* workshop

umbrella initiatives 109–10, 150
unconscious incompetence 155–6
Unilever 55–6
United States 52

values
   Hewlett Packard 102–3
   internalization of the vision 85–7
   PPR 125
   trust and 151–2
variance 133
vigilant consumer 55
Virgin Atlantic Airways 139
vision xv, xvi, 1–2, 3–4, 10–13
   characteristics of a good vision 11–13
   formulation *see* formulation of the
    vision
   House Model *see* House Model
Vision Express 20–1, 21–2
Vivendi Universal 41–3
Volvo 14, 51

Wal-Mart 3, 11, 12, 14
walking the talk 38
warning signals 37–8
Welch, Jack 83, 106–9, 121, 123, 150, 153
Westbrook, R. 9
working back from a projected point in
   the future 31
workshop 46–7, 62–8, 167
   action lists 76
   CEO role 67–8, 167
   input day 62–5
   participants 67
   second day 63, 65–7